Walking with God Through the Valley

Recovering the Purpose of Biblical Lament

May Young

An imprint of InterVarsity Press
Downers Grove, Illinois

InterVarsity Press
P.O. Box 1400 | Downers Grove, IL 60515-1426
ivpress.com | email@ivpress.com

©2025 by May Young

All rights reserved. No part of this book may be reproduced in any form without written permission from InterVarsity Press.

InterVarsity Press® is the publishing division of InterVarsity Christian Fellowship/USA®. For more information, visit intervarsity.org.

All Scripture quotations, unless otherwise indicated, are taken from The Holy Bible, New International Version®, NIV®. Copyright © 1973, 1978, 1984, 2011 by Biblica, Inc.™ Used by permission of Zondervan. All rights reserved worldwide. www.zondervan.com. The "NIV" and "New International Version" are trademarks registered in the United States Patent and Trademark Office by Biblica, Inc.™

While any stories in this book are true, some names and identifying information may have been changed to protect the privacy of individuals.

The publisher cannot verify the accuracy or functionality of website URLs used in this book beyond the date of publication.

Cover design: David Fassett
Interior design: Jeanna Wiggins
Images: © Abstract Aerial Art / DigitalVision / Getty Images, © Svetlana Repnitskaya / Moment / Getty Images

ISBN 978-1-5140-0396-1 (print) | ISBN 978-1-5140-0397-8 (digital)

Printed in the United States of America ∞

Library of Congress Cataloging-in-Publication Data
Names: Young, May, 1971- author.
Title: Walking with God through the valley : recovering the purpose of biblical lament / May Young.
Description: Downers Grove, IL : IVP Academic, [2025] | Includes bibliographical references and index.
Identifiers: LCCN 2024025665 (print) | LCCN 2024025666 (ebook) | ISBN 9781514003961 (print) | ISBN 9781514003978 (digital)
Subjects: LCSH: Laments in the Bible. | Laments. | BISAC: RELIGION / Biblical Studies / Old Testament / Poetry & Wisdom Literature | RELIGION / Christian Living / Spiritual Growth
Classification: LCC BS1199.L27 Y58 2025 (print) | LCC BS1199.L27 (ebook) | DDC 265/.85–dc23/eng/20240708
LC record available at https://lccn.loc.gov/2024025665
LC ebook record available at https://lccn.loc.gov/2024025666

"A fantastic book! Not only do we learn more about lament, but we are propelled through personal examples to practice lament individually and communally. May this book help the church recover lament as a central part of life with God."
Andrew Abernethy, professor of Old Testament at Wheaton College

"*Walking with God Through the Valley: Recovering the Purpose of Biblical Lament* is a carefully woven tapestry centered on an undervalued but oh-so essential thread of life—lament. Dr. Young skillfully amplifies the promised healing and liberation revealed when we lean into personal and communal lament. Readers will see that recovering biblical lament avails us to the healing, humility, and hindsight our soul longs to posture."
Lori E. Banfield, lecturer of psychology and practical theology at Eastern University and author of *Walking Worthy of My Calling: Journey Back to the Likeness of God*

"May Young's book speaks to the heart, the head, and the hands. This book shows how lament addresses a profound need in the church and in our lives to share our deepest and hardest feelings with God. Young combines meaningful stories of pain, loss, and hope with solid biblical insights about the history and theology of lament, its place in the Bible, and its purpose in our lives today. By offering reflection questions and suggestions for individual and corporate lament practices, every reader is encouraged to participate. This book will be a valuable gift to students and congregations alike!"
Beth Stovell, professor of Old Testament and chair of general theological studies at Ambrose University in Alberta, Canada

"In this stimulating and accessible study, May Young explores the misunderstood and underused genre of lament in the Bible with an eye to making lament come to life for both individuals and the corporate church as a whole. Drawing on her own personal experiences of loss, frustration, and anger, she shows that laments are not merely about 'sadness,' but that they can be a rich resource in many different situations, including sin and repentance, doubt, anger, loneliness, sickness and pain, death and loss. Her title well captures the running thread that she traces through the laments: that God walks with us throughout, and we are not alone. I highly recommend this book!"
David M. Howard, Jr., professor of Old Testament at Bethlehem College and Seminary in Minneapolis, Minnesota

"Dr. May Young has given us a rare book on lament in the Old Testament which is biblically grounded and pastorally wise. She writes not only as a scholar of the subject but also as a practitioner who shares movingly from her own experiences and those of fellow sufferers. Every spiritual leader should read this book to walk more closely with God in times of trouble!"
Jerry Hwang, associate professor of theology at Trinity Christian College

"This book is a captivating introduction to the concept of biblical lament. May Young achieves a brilliant feat in explaining to the reader—especially the reader unfamiliar with this concept—lament's nature, function, and purpose and the need for the practice of lament in the church today. Speaking from her heart, May shares snippets of her own experience and that of others in order to show how lament can bring people closer to God. Her pastoral concern and desire to help believers discover and embrace the power of lament in the midst of incomprehensible suffering is noticeable throughout the book."

Yacouba Sanon, assistant professor of Old Testament at Alliance Theological Seminary in Côte d'Ivoire in West Africa

"This is the book on lament that we've been waiting for and need. May Young merges her extensive study on biblical lament with profoundly personal applications for the individual and the community. The practice of lament is the missing link for many in healing from suffering, trauma, and pain. Young guides us through an understanding of biblical lament as a way forward, a guide to process with God the injustices and sorrows of life. Her work is timely, honest, and accessible."

Ingrid Faro, professor of Old Testament at Northern Seminary

"May Young's *Walking with God Through the Valley* makes a distinctive contribution to the literature on lament. Her sensitive, comprehensive look at the many faces of sorrow and suffering offers a fresh, accessible resource for dealing with times of anguish, both in our worshipping communities and in private devotions. Dr. Young's scholarship and depth of personal experience provide an insightful guide for dealing with the raw realities of life in a way that brings renewed understanding of God's goodness and steadfast love. Her book will benefit and encourage readers in both church and academy."

Dennis R. Magary, professor of Old Testament and Semitic languages at Trinity Evangelical Divinity School

"With a distinctive combination of academic expertise and pastoral sensitivity, Dr. May Young offers the church a great gift: an invitation and guide to the practice of lament. This is a clear, readable, and compassionate book, and it will offer comfort to those who are grieving and wisdom for those who walk alongside them."

Aubrey E. Buster, associate professor of Old Testament at Wheaton College

TO MY CHILDREN:

Deborah, Andrew, and Krissy.

I am so thankful for you!

Contents

Acknowledgments ix

1 Introduction 1

PART 1: HELPFUL CONTEXT FOR UNDERSTANDING BIBLICAL LAMENT

2 The Genre of Lament 15

3 Biblical Lament in the Ancient Near Eastern World 30

4 The Purpose of Lament 59

PART 2: PRACTICING LAMENT FOR VARIOUS SITUATIONS

5 Lament and Sin/Repentance 81

6 Lament and Doubt/Questions 99

7 Lament and Injustice/Unfair Circumstances and Anger 111

8 Lament and Loneliness/Abandonment 131

9 Lament and Sickness/Physical Pain 145

10 Lament and Death/Loss 159

11 Conclusion 181

Scripture Index 187

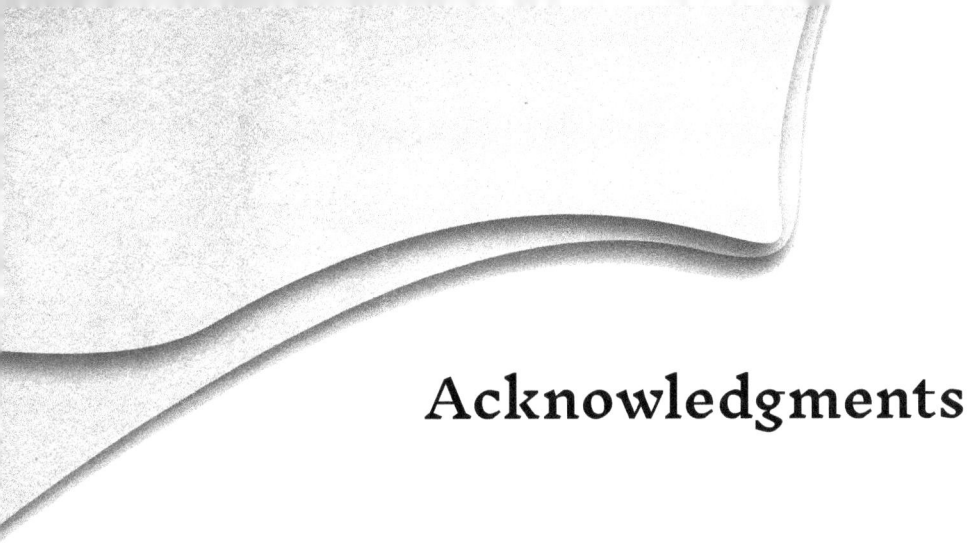

Acknowledgments

I would like to express my gratitude to all my family and friends who have supported me in the writing of this book. Your prayers and kind encouragement helped me tremendously throughout this process. This book would not have been possible without your love and support!

With deep gratitude!

1

Introduction

When I began my research as a biblical scholar, I had no idea that lament would be my area of interest. What could have been a gloomy topic ended up being one that sustained my soul through my own trying times. My interest in this topic began when I went through a personal trauma. I was a young wife with two small children, married to a pastor who was church planting. We struggled through ministry and other family obligations, but due to his unfaithfulness, I found myself feeling alone and abandoned. My life fell apart, and I was devastated.

It was through this experience that I learned about lament—a much-needed practice that sustained me through one of the most difficult times of my life. No one taught about lament in the church when I was growing up. Although I knew that life was not perfect and that we all go through trials, I was not equipped to face something so life changing and overwhelming. I did not know how to move on or process my feelings. I was broken and distressed to say the least. I could not eat or sleep for two weeks because I was so depressed. My life felt like a bad dream that I hoped would dissipate when I woke up the next morning, but when the morning came and my circumstances remained the same, I did not know what to do.

I felt abandoned, betrayed, lonely and lost, and the only solace I found was when I prayed and read the Bible. Sometimes my prayers were just tears and loud sobbing as I offered up my pain to God. Other times, I expressed my fears and anxiety about what the next steps were.

I found myself reading the Psalms incessantly because they gave voice to my pain and uncertainties. I cried out to the Lord in my loneliness, and the truth in the Bible gave me hope. However, like the psalmist in Psalms 42–43, I found my emotions vacillating. There were days I felt hopeful that better days were ahead and that the Lord was with me, and other days I mourned the loss of a marriage and the sadness of a broken family.

Through that period, I felt like I hit rock bottom, but much to my surprise, my lament did not lead me into an endless abyss of hopelessness. Rather, lament led me straight into the arms of God—my true Rock and foundation. I realized that he was with me in my pain. He was close to me when I had no one else. He understood my feelings of loneliness and abandonment. Even when I vacillated in my emotions, his presence was close. There were times when my doubts got the best of me, but I had to remember the truth in his word.

My journey was not linear but rather a winding path that gave me hope amid a broken world. The laments found in Scripture became the catalyst for the healing that my soul longed for. These prayers gave me permission to voice my pain to God and to wait on him even when I did not see any immediate change in my circumstances.

LAMENT FOR TODAY

As I continued my studies on lament and as I experienced healing power myself, I quickly realized that lament was not just something for my personal life behind closed doors. Rather, lament can serve as a healing agent for entire communities of people. We are living in a time of uncertainty, with increased feelings of anxiety and depression stemming from isolation, racial injustice, wars, an increase in gun violence, and political unrest. The current social climate not only has caused anxiety, depression, suffering, and grief but has also left us angry, confused, perplexed, and even numb about how to handle everything that is constantly bombarding our eyes, ears, and hearts.

While lament is found throughout Scripture, it seems that only recently has the church recalled its importance. When I began teaching at Taylor

University, a Christian liberal arts university in Upland, Indiana, I spoke about lament in several of my classes. Each time, several students confided that this was their first exposure to this concept or that they had not heard much teaching on lament in their own churches. While there has been an increased awareness of lament in the past few years, many still do not know how to practice lament or why it is important for our whole selves.

Furthermore, there is skepticism about lament in some spaces. I have even spoken to some Christians who view lament as antithetical to faith or confidence in God. Questions still abound: Is it not wrong to question, doubt, or wallow in grief? Does it not just exhibit weak faith? Is lament just being sad? Why do we need to keep rehearsing our pain? What exactly is lament? How does it help? How do we actually practice lament in our personal lives or as a community? These are just some of the questions and sentiments that have been raised.

DEFINING TERMS

Lament can be broadly understood as "expressing the reality of suffering," or more specifically expressing what one feels in the midst of pain.[1] These expressions are demonstrated through various means or practices. To be sure, the practice of lament and the concept of lament are not necessarily equivalent, however, because individual practices give form to the concept of lament, I will be referring to them interchangeably.

Of course, one does not have to be a Christian to lament, but the concept and practice of *biblical* lament goes beyond the general understanding of merely expressing the reality of suffering. Too often lament is viewed as a practice or end in itself. Some have even become stuck in their pain as they continued to rehearse their suffering. Although this book does encompass the general nature of lament—that is, the expression of the reality of pain—its main focus is on biblical lament, which is rooted in the foundational understanding of the lament genre found in Scripture. As we study lament, it is important to distinguish between lament as a

---

[1]Samuel E. Balentine, *Prayer in the Hebrew Bible: The Drama of Divine-Human Dialogue* (Minneapolis: Fortress, 1993), 150.

genre or type of literature in the Bible and the practice or concept of biblical lament. Understanding the genre of lament in the Bible will help us in our practice.

WHAT IS BIBLICAL LAMENT? UNDERSTANDING HOW GENRE INFORMS OUR PRACTICE

While the Bible describes people lamenting—for example, Job (Job 3), Jeremiah (Jer 11:18-20), Habakkuk (Hab 1), and Paul (2 Cor 12:8)—it also features a specific lament genre, or type of literature, which is found primarily in the Psalms. This genre is composed of prayers that are characterized by a specific form with common elements. In chapter three we will discuss these elements and the lament genre in detail as well as examine how the Hebrew terms for lament are used in the Bible. Understanding these common elements will help clarify how biblical lament is a much deeper process than just expressing our suffering. Chapter four will explore how lament as a genre in the Bible is similar to and different from the lament of other societies in the ancient Near East. These distinctions offer further guidance for the practice of biblical lament in our own lives.

At its most basic level, the practice of lament offers a way for us to process suffering, injustice, pain, and disappointments because we live in a broken and fallen world. Instead of avoiding these disappointments and hurts, lament helps us to engage these pains so we can move forward. Unfortunately, we live in a context that is great at avoiding conflict and discomfort. Instead of dealing with our pain, we numb it with busyness or entertainment. We would rather spend hours surfing the internet, scrolling through social media, distracting ourselves with retail therapy, binging on Netflix, playing video games, or participating in other addictive habits rather than facing the pain, anger, confusion, and loneliness we carry in our hearts. Some even turn to other, more self-destructive behaviors such as drugs, alcohol, and other addictions to quell these troublesome feelings or silence the pain. It is no wonder that the World Health Organization reports that more than 300 million people worldwide are estimated to live with depression, and adults are not the only ones dealing with stressors.² When surveyed in 2017, 40 percent of teens reported feeling irritable or angry within the past month, and over a third reported feeling nervous, anxious, or overwhelmed.³ As these numbers continue to skyrocket after a worldwide pandemic, is there any hope for us moving forward? How are we to cope with these bleak statistics? Are we destined to live our lives bogged down by anxiety and depression?

Psychologists affirm that the healthiest way to move forward is to feel our feelings. Failure to do so could result in negative consequences for not just our mental health but also our physical health.⁴ A twelve-year follow-up study found that the suppression of emotions may lead to earlier death, including death from cancer.⁵ This correlation between our emotions and physical health reinforces that we are whole persons who engage life emotionally, physically, and spiritually. How we process our pain, doubts, questions, and anger will inevitably affect our emotional, physical, and spiritual well-being.

The practice of lament found in the Bible is ultimately an act of faith. When we face struggles, our instinct is usually to turn away from God or shut down, but lament encourages us to press in and engage God even in our brokenness and despair. This instinct to retreat from God is evident early in the Bible. After the fall, Adam and Eve hide from God instead of turning to him—perhaps because of doubt, pride, sin, shame, or the pain of disappointing God, or perhaps all of these. As we continue to live in this broken world, these same factors have also influenced our own desire

---

²World Health Organization, "Depression and Other Common Mental Disorders: Global Health Estimates," 2017, https://iris.who.int/bitstream/handle/10665/254610/WHO-MSD-MER-2017.2-eng.pdf?sequence=1.

³Kathleen Smith, "6 Common Triggers of Teen Stress," Psycom, updated October 21, 2022, www.psycom.net/common-triggers-teen-stress.

⁴This study examines the correlation between anger, anxiety, and depression and cardiovascular disease. While the findings show that the overlap of all three may lead to a disposition toward negative affectivity, their research cites an extensive list of studies that have researched these correlations. Jerry Suls and James Bunde, "Anger, Anxiety, and Depression as Risk Factors for Cardiovascular Disease: The Problems and Implication of Overlapping Affective Dispositions," *Psychological Bulletin* 131, no. 2 (2005): 260-300.

⁵Benjamin P. Chapman, Kevin Fiscella, Ichiro Kawachi, Paul Duberstein, and Peter Muennig, "Emotion Suppression and Mortality Risk over a 12-Year Follow-Up," *Journal of Psychosomatic Research* 75, no. 4 (October 2014): 381-85. See also Philip J. Quartana and John W. Burns, "Emotion Suppression Affects Cardiovascular Responses to Initial and Subsequent Laboratory Stressors," *Journal of Health Psychology* 15, no. 3 (September 2010): 511-28.

to turn away from God during difficult times. Unfortunately, I have heard countless stories from friends and others who left the church or stopped praying when they experienced deep pain, doubts, anger, and disappointments in their lives. Instead of dealing with these issues, they retreated from others, including God. Many in times of crisis have even declared that the Christian life just did not work for them. In other words, they did not feel that the Bible or God had much to offer when they faced challenging situations.

Are they right? What does the Bible have to offer us when we are suffering? Too often, many just quote Romans 8:28, "And we know that in all things God works for the good of those who love him, who have been called according to his purpose." Does this mean we need to be people who grin and bear all circumstances? After all, God is working all things for the good of those who love him. Is there no room for struggle or doubt? I have heard of people who lost children to terrible accidents, only to face church members who told them that even in this, God had a purpose. At the time, they were definitely not comforted by this thought. Instead, many wanted to shut down and not engage further with such insensitive statements. While God may have an ultimate purpose for this seemingly senseless loss, quoting this verse only exhibits a callousness to suffering and pain.

Thankfully, the Bible has so much more to say than Romans 8:28. We are not called to a stoic acceptance of life's pain and hurts but rather engagement with God in the midst of these dark valleys. Instead of moving away or disengaging, lament invites God into our doubts, pain, and struggle, setting us on a path to become people of resilience. Often we mistakenly think that we can overcome our pain and doubts without ever truly facing them. But they do not just disappear because we do not acknowledge them. Instead, we need to do the hard work of feeling and working through these dark thoughts in order for us to move forward and grow. Through the practice of lament, we are able to be a people of God filled with hope and resilience. When we press into our pain in the presence of God, we are reminded that we are not alone. As the psalmist recognized, "Even though I walk through the valley of the shadow of death, I will fear no evil, for you are with me" (Ps 23:4 ESV). The only way we can truly find healing and strength to move forward is when we turn to God and acknowledge his presence as we face pain, confusion, and doubt.

THE STATE OF LAMENT IN THE CHURCH

Why is it that churches so often fail to model this critical practice for the life of the church? When I was growing up, most individuals in the church did not share their painful experiences while they were going through their dark valleys. What they shared were the triumphs after the difficulties had passed and they saw God's faithfulness. Why do we hear so many stories about those who have overcome difficulties only *after* they have experienced victory? Sometimes we were not even aware that they were struggling. Why do we not hear from Christian believers and their testimonies while they are *in the midst of* their pain and suffering?

To be sure, it is inspiring to hear about those who have overcome very difficult circumstances, but why does hardly anyone share the struggles that led to these victorious outcomes? This lack of transparency inevitably creates a culture of triumphalism with little room for deep struggle and doubt. Perhaps this precedent has contributed to our unwillingness to practice lament and be honest about our pain when we are going through difficulties, both individually and collectively. Perhaps this has also contributed to feelings of isolation when we are struggling.

When authenticity is promoted in the church, many do not want to be vulnerable for fear of judgment and feeling humiliated by others. Some people, when they voiced their struggles in the church, received pat answers and were expected to overcome these issues in a timely fashion. Sadly, what ends up happening is that when people face hardship, the last place they want to be is in the church. Many have even abandoned their faith because they did not see God working or bringing the same victorious outcome that others testified to. There are also those who feel that their struggle is taking too long to overcome and have become disheartened. These patterns cause us to hide our difficulties because we are afraid that we would appear weak in faith. The judgments of those around us often lead us to portray an artificial strength that God never called us to display. In its haste to communicate the triumphant message of Jesus, the church inadvertently communicates that to experience loss, sadness, and grief is to be a failure.

While we can all think of stories where there was no room for grief and sadness, it is important to note that statistics also corroborate these experiences. A study by Lifeway Research reveals that 59 percent of those with mental health challenges and 65 percent of family members of those with mental health challenges want their church to talk more openly about their struggles.[6] When we do not openly discuss mental health and other difficulties, a triumphalist culture in the church is reinforced. The church becomes a place to put our best foot forward. This should not be the case. The church is the body of Christ. As Paul exhorts, "If one member suffers, all suffer together; if one member is honored, all rejoice together" (1 Cor 12:26 ESV). We should be just as comfortable sharing in one another's suffering as we are rejoicing over one another's triumphs.

Even while noting the value of lament, it needs to be noted that lament is not a substitute for professional health care. While it is important to recognize that lamenting is more than just airing our complaints or wallowing in our despair, it is not a magic bullet that will cure us of all our mental health issues and does not replace therapy or other treatments prescribed by licensed professionals. It is important to seek out professional mental health care when appropriate. While some treatments may incorporate aspects of the practice of lament, mental health issues are complex and often require additional important expertise, which I will not address due to the focus of this book.

My experience with students and personal reflection on the church has made me aware of the importance of understanding and exploring what the Bible teaches about lament. While it has been encouraging to see many advocating for lament recently, there is so much more for us to glean from Scripture and scholarship on this topic.

---

[6]Bob Smietana, "Mental Illness Remains Taboo Topic for Many Pastors," Lifeway Research, September 22, 2014, https://research.lifeway.com/2014/09/22/mental-illness-remains-taboo-topic-for-many-pastors/.

CORPORATE LAMENT

Until now, I have spoken about lament mainly as something we can practice as individuals. Lament, however, is also necessary for the corporate body. While pain is often felt individually, it always has implications for those around us, both for how the sufferer interacts with the community and how the community responds to the sufferer. It is unfortunate that many have found the church to be a callous place when they are suffering. Many are at a loss as to how to respond to those who are suffering, so instead of engaging, we just avoid those who are struggling in order to minimize awkwardness. But we need to heed the popular adage that the church is to be a hospital for those in pain, not a museum for saints. Lamenting together as a body of Christ will help us move closer to actualizing this ideal. Especially amid our current context, the church needs to be a healing presence for the world.

Among other things, corporate lament offers an opportunity for us to stand alongside those who are hurting. We when practice lament corporately, we are giving witness to the pain and suffering of our fellow brothers and sisters. Suffering and pain are part of the fallen world in which we live. Acknowledging this fact is not a sign of defeat. In our acknowledgment, we are facing these realities with truth. This process offers a path for us to move from despair to resilience.

Corporate lament also encompasses times when the church as a community must come together in response to suffering or injustice that surrounds us. As we will see in chapter two, the communal lament prayers in the Bible are in the context of suffering experienced by the community collectively. Such situations require us to wait on God together. Sometimes communal lament can be quite uncomfortable because we do not have the answer to the problems and pervasive evil around us, but it fosters authentic community. In discussing Lamentations 5, the final chapter of Lamentations and the only communal lament, Kathleen O'Connor notes that the ending of the book

> expresses the community's doubt about God's care and about God's character. It utters the unthinkable—that God has utterly and permanently

rejected them, cast them off in unrelenting anger.... Such is the ending of this book, and I think it is wonderful. It is wonderful because it is truthful, because it does not force hope prematurely, because it expresses what many in worlds of trauma and destruction know to be true.[7]

Corporate lament calls us together to engage God in truth, humility, and waiting. Perhaps we have lost this focus in our churches today.

THE ROAD MAP FOR DISCUSSION

The remainder of the book will be divided into two main sections. The first section will introduce some basic categories and context for understanding lament in the Bible, for example, explaining the difference between individual versus corporate lament. Additionally, this section will discuss the different facets of the lament genre that move beyond the mere expression of sadness. As we explore the lament genre, we will see how these examples help to inform our practice of lament and the process of lamenting. There is greater depth and dimensions to lament than just the typical caricature of sadness. We will also investigate the difference between laments in the Bible compared those in the ancient Near Eastern context and address the theological and theoretical reasons for the purpose of lament.

The second main section of this book will explore some specific laments within this genre to see how they inform us about a variety of situations including doubt, anxiety, injustice, and grief. While many think that lament as a genre is focused mainly on feeling sorrow or sadness, the Bible shows us that lament encompasses a greater range of emotions. In fact, the biblical authors lament a variety of situations and circumstances. Early Christian monk and theologian John Cassian (AD 380) observed,

> Not every kind of shedding of tears is produced by one feeling or virtue. For in one way does that weeping originate that is caused by pricks of our sins striking our heart.... There is too another kind of tears, which are caused not by knowledge of one's self but by the hardness and sins of

---

[7]Kathleen O'Connor, *Lamentations and the Tears of the World* (Maryknoll, NY: Orbis Books, 2004), 88.

others. . . . And these (tears) were certainly not caused by the same as those that arise in Psalm 6 from the person of the penitent but were due to the anxieties of life and its distresses and losses, by which the righteous who are living in this world are oppressed.[8]

This is important to highlight as we consider the practice of lament and the various contexts of lament in Scripture. If we fail to recognize the broad spectrum of lament, we will have a limited understanding of why this practice is important for our Christian faith. To be sure, sadness is an important part of lament, but this is only a portion of what we see in the Bible. Highlighting these differences in the biblical genre of lament will help to broaden our understanding of the process of lament both individually and collectively.

This second half of the book will also discuss lamenting in the context of six broad categories with examples from the biblical genre of lament alongside personal testimonies of individuals who have practiced lament in difficult times. Chapter five will focus on lament in the context of sin and repentance. We often see this in the clarion call of the prophets to the people of Israel and Judah. They were called to lament their sins and return to Yahweh, who loved them, and this point has significance for our own contexts as well. Chapter six deals with lament in the midst of doubt and questions. The Bible gives us examples of godly people who questioned God and even doubted his goodness. As we will see, God is not afraid of our questions and doubts. Chapter seven will explore how lament helps us when we face anger, injustice, and unfair circumstances. God is the ultimate judge, and we can bring our case to him. Honesty of expression in these circumstances helps us to deal with emotions that can sometime overwhelm us. Lament also helps us when we deal with loneliness and abandonment. Chapter eight will show us that we are not alone in this struggle; the psalmist also wrestles with such thoughts. In chapter nine we will turn our attention to the experience of sickness and physical pain. Lament may be especially applicable for those struggling with

---

[8]Dean O. Wenthe and Thomas C. Oden, eds., *Jeremiah, Lamentations*, Ancient Christian Commentary on Scripture 12 (Downers Grove, IL: InterVarsity Press, 2009), 539.

chronic pain or other physical ailments. Lastly, in chapter ten we will consider lament in the context of death and loss. As we can see, these topics will touch on some relevant circumstances that require practical guidance. These chapters will explore how the practice of lament, informed through biblical lament, is an appropriate response not just for individuals but also for the church as the body of Christ.

There is much more to explore on each of these topics in our lives before God. The purpose of this book is to begin the conversation and to show that lament is a deeply rooted biblical concept. As we journey together, we will see that the Bible has a great deal to offer us regarding the practice of lament that will shape not just our individual lives but the churches and communities in which we find ourselves.

PART 1

Helpful Context for Understanding Biblical Lament

2

The Genre of Lament

Scripture, especially Psalms and Lamentations, provides our primary corpora for the genre of lament, which we will be examining more closely in this chapter.[1] But before we begin, it is important to point out the distinction between the genre of lament and specific Hebrew terms referring to lament. Most of these terms are more closely associated with ritual mourning of death and destruction than with general situations of pain and suffering. The three most common Hebrew words for lament are *qînâ* (noun), deriving from *qîn* (verb); *ʾēvel* (noun), from *ʾāval* (verb); and *mispēd* (noun), from *sāpad* (verb). These terms are used most often to refer to a ritual, dirge, or mourning for the deceased. They are also used literally or figuratively to describe lament over the destruction of a nation or city. Most occurrences of these terms focus mainly on mourning rituals or associated outward mourning acts. More specifically, the most common term associated with lament (*qînâ*, or in the plural *qînôt*) technically refers to a biblical funeral dirge or a eulogy and is therefore used in contexts such as 2 Samuel 1:17, where David writes a *qînâ* for Saul and Jonathan, or in 2 Samuel 3:33, where he writes one for Abner. The term is also used to lament the destruction of a city, such as Tyre in Ezekiel 27:32. These terms highlight the difference between a dirge, which mourns the deceased, and the broader concepts associated with lament. Dirges are

---

[1] Laments are also found in other Old Testament books, e.g., Jeremiah, Job, Habakkuk, Ezekiel; and in the New Testament, e.g., Jn 11:17-32; 12:1-7; Mk 15:34; Mt 27:45-46; but discussions on the development of this form will focus on the Old Testament, especially the Psalms.

not trying to change a situation. They mourn the death of something in the past. This is clearly different from laments (both individual and communal) in Psalms, which often look forward to the hope of rescue. R. W. L. Moberly rightly notes that even though these dirges and laments are distinct in the Bible, nevertheless "the usage of the term lament to depict the content of the relevant psalms, in which the psalmist cries out to God in time of trouble, seems entirely appropriate."[2]

With this in mind, two questions come to the fore. What are the differences between individual lament and corporate/communal lament in terms of genre? Are these genres just general in nature, or can they be instructive for specific situations? This chapter will discuss the characteristic elements of biblical lament in detail, because we cannot recover the biblical practice of lament if we do not know what characterizes the laments we find in Scripture. Thus, we dive into the study of Scripture, so we can learn the nature of lament for God's people.

Distinguishing between form and content is fundamental here. More specifically, we need to recognize that while the lament genre deals with content or issues that are common to humanity, it does so in a particular way or through specific forms. In general, prayers of lament often deal with, for example, sickness, oppression by enemies, abandonment by God, sin, loneliness, betrayal, mental anguish, and even death. Many if not all these topics are still relevant today. The most basic way to view these laments is to see them as prayer songs that were originally spoken and eventually written or developed over time by individuals or communities dealing with suffering. These songs provide a glimpse into their life of faith. Moberly rightly notes,

> The predominance of laments at the heart of Israel's prayers means that problems that give rise to lament are not something marginal or unusual but rather are central to the life of faith. Moreover, they show that the experiences of anguish and puzzlement in the life of faith is not a sign of deficient faith, something to be outgrown or put behind one, but rather is intrinsic to the very nature of faith.[3]

---

[2] R. W. L. Moberly, "Lament," in *New International Dictionary of Old Testament Theology and Exegesis*, ed. Willem A. VanGemeren (Grand Rapids, MI: Zondervan, 1997), 4:867.
[3] Moberly, "Lament," 879.

The Genre of Lament

As was also the case in biblical times, prayers are expressed both orally and in written form. Often the written forms are created to preserve the original, which is central to our discussion of biblical lament. Carleen Mandolfo states that the laments "in the Bible are most likely a secondary form, written down in order to preserve a memory of an originary ritual."[4] Therefore, while the themes in these expressions of lament are universal, how the written prayers took shape was particular to different ancient Near Eastern cultures. These forms or genres have distinct patterns, functions, and themes.[5] Topically, biblical laments are not that different from those of other ancient Near Eastern cultures, whether Egyptian, Sumerian, Hittite, or Babylonian. Specific differences and similarities between Israel's prayers of lament and those of its ancient Near Eastern neighbors will be addressed in chapter three. The rest of this chapter will explore the genre of lament found in the Old Testament, especially in Psalms.

HISTORICAL DEVELOPMENT OF THE LAMENT GENRE

Hermann Gunkel's work in the early twentieth century on Psalms, or what some refer to as the Psalter, was seminal for our understanding of the different literary forms or genres found in the Bible.[6] When he was reading through the Old Testament, especially Psalms, Gunkel recognized that many of the prayers had similar themes and shared similar structures, style, rhetorical features, terms, and even images. He noticed repetition of specific elements in the different types of psalms and was able to identify four main types among these prayer songs: individual laments, communal (corporate) laments, descriptive praises (hymns), and declarative praises (thanksgiving psalms).[7] He also recognized that these categories were not

---

[4] Carleen Mandolfo, "Language of Lament in the Psalms," in *The Oxford Handbook of the Psalms*, ed. William P. Brown (Oxford: Oxford University Press, 2014), 114. An originary ritual refers to the original lament practice, not the literary form.

[5] According to Merriam-Webster, genre is "a category of artistic, musical or literary composition characterized by a particular style, form or content" (*Merriam-Webster's Collegiate Dictionary*). www.merriam-webster.com/dictionary/genre. Genre is important because it helps us to identify the type of literature we are reading, which helps to set expectations and assist us in our understanding of the content. For example, we do not read fairy tales the same way we would read biographies.

[6] Hermann Gunkel, *The Psalms: A Form-Critical Introduction* (Philadelphia: Fortress, 1967).

[7] Gunkel, *Psalms*, 30-35. These are not the only genres he identifies. He also observes royal psalms as well as entrance liturgies and other minor literary types. Gunkel's work laid the foundation for

always clear cut. Mixture of forms as well as transformation over time was also noted. Additionally, Gunkel identified other minor forms.

The identification of these four main categories was helpful in discussing both the content and structure of prayers in the Psalter. Since Gunkel's seminal work, there has been much more discussion of these and other genres found in the Old Testament, especially Psalms.[8] This literary approach to scholarship on the Psalms sought to identify not only the forms or genre but also any ceremonies, rituals, or life situations (German *Sitz im Leben*) associated with them.[9] By identifying these associations, scholars hoped to provide insight into how these prayer songs originated and developed as well as their function.[10] It is thought that these psalms functioned in both the religious and social life of ancient Israel. For example, Psalms 2; 18; 20–21; 45; 72; 101; 110; 132; 144:1-11 are identified as royal psalms concerned entirely with kings, most likely used during royal celebrations and religious festivals that were organized by the Israelite kings.[11] While Gunkel recognized that many psalms could have had functions or ceremonies associated with them, he also believed that they were later liberated from their ceremonial settings to be independent spiritual songs and prayers.[12]

---

the area of biblical form criticism, which was interested in identifying the genres and function of these songs in their original context.

[8]The following are just a few examples of form critical-analysis and research that built on Gunkel's work: Claus Westermann, *Praise and Lament in the Psalms* (Atlanta: John Knox, 1981); Sigmund Mowinckel, *The Psalms in Israel's Worship* (Leiden: Brill, 1962); Walter Brueggemann, *The Psalms and the Life of Faith* (Minneapolis: Fortress, 1995); Craig C. Broyles, *The Conflict of Faith and Experience in the Psalms* (Sheffield, UK: JSOT Press, 1989); Marvin A. Sweeney and Ehud Ben Zvi, eds., *The Changing Face of Form Criticism for the Twenty-First Century* (Grand Rapids, MI: Eerdmans, 2003).

[9]For more information on the genre and original context or settings of individual psalms, see Erhard S. Gerstenberger: *Psalms, Part 1: An Introduction to Cultic Poetry* (Grand Rapids, MI: Eerdmans, 1988); *Psalms, Part 2 and Lamentations* (Grand Rapids, MI: Eerdmans, 2001).

[10]See Erhard S. Gerstenberger, "Life Situations and Theological Concepts of Old Testament Psalms," *Old Testament Essays* 18 (2005): 82-92.

[11]Hermann Gunkel, *Introduction to Psalms: The Genres of the Religious Lyric of Israel* (Macon, GA: Mercer University Press, 1998), 99-100.

[12]Gunkel, *Psalms, Part 1*, viii. Claus Westermann also notes that laments changed from the earlier to later periods. In the later periods, the complaint against God as a feature of the psalm is almost completely gone. "The exact opposite appeared, viz., the justification of God's righteousness or simply praise of the righteous God. Nevertheless . . . the perplexity at the incomprehensive judgments of God remained" (Westermann, *Praise and Lament*, 171-72). For additional discussion on the emergence of penitential prayer found in the narrative accounts of the Persian period that

In general, the two types of lament (individual and corporate/communal) comprise about one-third of Psalms, which means there are more laments than any other types of psalms in this book.[13] This may be surprising because we often associate Psalms with praises or hymns. Perhaps this proportion is a realistic reflection of life, which is often filled with difficulty and hardships.

The Old Testament emphasizes that Yahweh is the one who saves and brings deliverance from affliction. Over and over again, the people of Israel received deliverance when they cried out to him in their distress. These lament prayers are not arbitrary and disorganized. While there are variations depending on the context, lament psalms in general display a fixed structure with common elements. These elements do not always appear in the same order, nor do all the psalms of lament contain every component listed, but nevertheless scholars have identified some shared similarities.[14]

This is a very important point when we are trying to understand what characterizes the biblical lament genre. More specifically, we are asking why we refer to certain prayers as laments as opposed to others. What distinguishes them from other types of literature or genres? Sometimes people think that the biblical laments are solely expressions that pour out sadness and pain before the Lord. We do not necessarily associate any structure with these types of prayers. While it is important not to discount the honest, raw cries that are common in these laments, we also want to recognize that these prayers have common essential elements, which can be instructive for our own practice of lament.

---

placed greater emphasis on the recognition of sin, see Mark J. Boda, "The Priceless Gain of Penitence: From Communal Lament to Penitential Prayer in the 'Exilic' Liturgy of Israel," *Horizons in Biblical Theology* 25 (2003): 51-75.

[13] Gunkel, *Introduction to Psalms*. Gunkel lists the following as communal laments: Ps 44; (58); 74; 79; 80; 83; (106); (125); Lam 5 (see page 82 in Gunkel). The following 39 psalms are categorized by Gunkel as individual laments: Ps 3; 5–7; 13; 17; 22; 25–26; 27:7-14; 28; 31; 35; 38–39; 42–43; 51; 54–57; 59; 61; 63–64; 69–71; 86; 88; 102; 109; 120; 130; 140–143; Lam 3 (see page 121 in Gunkel). Because genre is not always clear cut, the actual number varies among different scholars. For example, Carleen Mandolfo lists a total of 42 psalms of lament (Ps 3–7; 11; 13; 17; 22–23; 27–28; 30–32; 35; 38–39; 41; 44; 51; 57; 60; 63; 69; 71; 74; 77; 79–80; 83; 85; 88; 90–91; 94; 102–103; 123; 126; 130; 137). Thirty of these are categorized as individual laments, and the remaining twelve as communal/corporate (Mandolfo, "Language of Lament," 115, 127).

[14] For some additional examples, see Westermann, *Praise and Lament*, 64; William H. Bellinger Jr., *Psalms: A Guide to Studying the Psalter* (Grand Rapids, MI: Baker Academic, 2012), 65-66.

Perhaps the best way to understand this topic is to think about how we study the Lord's Prayer (Mt 6:9-13; Lk 11:1-4). Often in a sermon or teaching on this prayer, the preacher or teacher breaks down the different elements that make up this prayer. For instance, the phrase "Our Father, who art in heaven" emphasizes that this prayer is directed to our Heavenly Father, not a God who is emotionally distant or has no personal relationship with us. However, unlike our earthly fathers, he is in heaven and can accomplish more than any earthly father. Each component of the Lord's Prayer can be analyzed to give us insight into how we should be praying. After all, this is the model Jesus gave to his disciples when they asked him to teach them about prayer. While some of us recite the Lord's Prayer by heart, many of us also personalize the elements in this prayer to assist us when we pray. In other words, we use the Lord's Prayer as a model but fill in the details with our own specifics. Similarly, when we study the components of lament, we are also learning to practice lament in a biblical way.

The following are the essential parts that make up individual and corporate laments:[15]

- address or invocation
- lamentation/petition/complaint
- motivations
- confession of trust and assurance of being heard
- vow of praise

Address or invocation. The first element in a biblical lament is usually an address to the Lord. This is often the first words of the prayer. Many times, the psalmist will refer to God's name (e.g., Ps 9:2; 54:1) or his character (e.g., righteousness and faithfulness; Ps 4:1; 143:1). The importance of this component is that the psalmist is turning to God. This is a critical starting point because lament is based on relationship. Walter Brueggemann describes lament as dialogical, indicating that prayers of

---

[15]Westermann, *Praise and Lament*, 265; Brueggemann, *Psalms and the Life*, 70. This list combines those provided by Westermann and Brueggemann. Individual and corporate laments also have their particular distinctions, which I will discuss later.

lament are not just words spoken in a vacuum. They are spoken to God, the very one who can enact change. These prayers are addressed to God, with whom we have a relationship. As New Testament believers, we can approach his throne with confidence because of Jesus (Heb 4:16). Turning to God instead of turning away or isolating ourselves in our pain is the first step in the practice of biblical lament.

Lamentation/petition/complaint. This next component can be considered the actual lament. It can include expressions of anguish, pain, hurt, anger, or even accusations against God or others. Generally, the lament may be as a result of sickness (e.g., Ps 6:2), injustice (e.g., Ps 73:4-10), personal sin (e.g., Ps 51:1-3), death (e.g., Ps 88:3-9), attacks from enemies (e.g., Ps 59:1-4), loneliness and abandonment (e.g., Ps 31:11-12), or shame and humiliation (e.g., Ps 69:19-20). This component highlights the honesty conveyed through the prayer. Depending on the context, the psalmist expresses raw pain, fear, danger, distress, disappointment, confusion, doubt, hatred, or even anger. This aspect is perhaps what we most closely associate with the idea of lament. Here the psalmists express their true feelings. They take off their masks and are vulnerable before the Lord.

This section may also include complaints against enemies or even against the Lord. There is an important distinction between complaint in the context of a lament and merely grumbling or complaining. The wilderness generation in Exodus 15–17 and Numbers 14–17 was condemned because they were grumbling and complaining against the leadership and against the Lord *to one another*. In other words, their complaints were not prayers. They were not bringing their thoughts in prayer before the Lord. This is an important distinction because complaint against God to others is condemned, but bringing complaints to the Lord is encouraged. For the wilderness generation, grumbling to others was just a way to express what they believed to be true about God. It was not dialogical, only a way to air out their grievances and unbelief. Tremper Longman III rightly observes, "Whereas those rebels complained about God to each other, the psalmists (and Job) voice their laments directly to God. The latter indicates that they have not given up on God or abandoned hope that God would eventually answer their prayers."[16] We must distinguish between self-focused expressions of self-pity or frustration and prayers directed to the one who has the power to bring about change. We do not have to hide our true feelings or complaints from the Lord. Like Habakkuk or Job, we can bring our complaints and questions to God. Instead of stuffing down these emotions, lament reminds us that God is there to process them with us. Similarly, when we are honest through complaints or questions with a loved one, we often grow closer in our relationship. It is through the messiness of this process that we can break down barriers and grow in the relationship. We want those closest to us to express their true feelings, even if they are not pleasant to hear, because it helps promote greater intimacy. Instead of telling or complaining to others about us or stewing over their thoughts, we desire for them to speak honestly with us. Bringing our laments, complaints, and petitions before God functions in the same way.

Motivations. This component in lament often flows out of the lamentation/petition/complaint. It gives reasons for God to act or move toward action. These actions range from protection and salvation (e.g., Ps 86:1-4), forgiving sins (e.g., Ps 25:11), healing sickness (e.g., Ps 6:2-4), to judging and dealing with enemies (e.g., Ps 7:6). Oftentimes this part of lament is an appeal to God's own reputation and name (e.g., Ps 25:11), God's past action or deliverance (e.g., Ps 22:4-5), the psalmist's innocence (e.g., Ps 17:1-5), the psalmist's helplessness (e.g., Ps 69:1), or the psalmist's trust (e.g., Ps 57:1). This element connects the requests with what the psalmist knows to be true about God and his character. By reciting these truths about God, the psalmist is reminding himself that he is approaching a God who cares and who has revealed himself in the past. Recalling God's character and works provides the psalmist confidence to ask God to act again in accordance with his character and lovingkindness.

Lament is not just coming before God in honesty and vulnerability; we need to remember who God is. What does the Bible tell us about God?

---

[16]Tremper Longman III, "From Weeping to Rejoicing: Psalm 150 as the Conclusion to the Psalter," in *The Psalms: Language for All Seasons of the Soul*, ed. Andrew M. Schmutzer and David M. Howard Jr. (Chicago: Moody, 2014), 219.

What promises can we claim as believers in the midst of struggle or pain? How has God worked in the past, both in the Bible and in our own lives? We must spend time reflecting on these things. Like the psalmist, we can also remind God of his promises and his character. We can cry out to him to hear our prayers and to see our pain. We can ask for his forgiveness and mercy. We can appeal to his justice because of his character. These are all part of the process of lament. We are not just rehearsing our pains; instead, we are bringing what we know to be true about God into our darkest moments. When we are walking in the valley, we can't let our pain blind us to what we know to be true about God. Our pain can make us nearsighted, but reflecting on these aspects of God can help us step back and gain a greater perspective.

Confession of trust and assurance of being heard. This element is important in that it marks the shift from lament to hope. More specifically, it is the turning point from distress to trust in the psalmist. Often this is indicated through the vocabulary of the psalmist. In Hebrew grammar, this is called a *vav* adversative (or *waw* adversative), which is translated through the conjunction *vav*, "but" or "now" (e.g., Ps 55:16, 23). Claus Westermann notes, "The *waw* adversative combined with the subject at the beginning of the clause indicates that here something else begins. . . . They indicate a transition from lamentation to another mode of speech, the confession of trust or the assurance of being heard."[17]

The confession of trust and the assurance of being heard are not synonymous. While they are distinct components, generally there is not a clear boundary between the two, and thus it makes more sense to refer to them together. For instance, the confession of trust may be the result of the assurance of being heard, and sometimes the psalmist mentions one while leaving out the other.

This shift from lament to hope has perplexed scholars, and many have investigated this change.[18] While there is no definitive answer for how this

---

[17]Westermann, *Praise and Lament*, 71-72. Not all transitions are marked by the *vav* adversative (e.g., Ps 17:15).

[18]See Federico G. Villanueva, *The "Uncertainty of a Hearing": A Study of the Sudden Change of Mood in the Psalms of Lament* (Leiden: Brill, 2008), 2-27.

shift occurs, it is important to recognize that this change does exist. Perhaps the earliest and most prominent view on the nature of this shift comes from Joachim Begrich, who proposed that these transitions indicate the coming intervention of God to the individual through an oracle of salvation by a prophet or priest (e.g., Ps 60:6-8; 81:6-10; 109:7-9).[19] However, Westermann indicates that these oracles of salvation are hardly ever referred to in the book of Psalms, though they occur frequently in the prophetic books (e.g., Is 33:10-13). Therefore, John Wevers argues that the insufficient examples of these oracles from the Psalms makes this view questionable. Instead, he proposes that the use of the divine name Yahweh as a vocative along with an imperative verb indicates that there was thought to be power in the use of the name, which gave the psalmist confidence (e.g., Ps 20:7).[20]

A recent essay by Daniel Estes argues that Wevers's view is too narrow to explain the psychological transition evident within psalms. Instead, Estes argues that the transformation from pain into praise results from the psalmists' meditation on the works of God, his character, and his word (e.g., Ps 1:2; 9:8; 77:12). "As the psalmists contemplate these theological truth, their view of their adversities is altered as the process of meditation causes them to perceive their experience through the lens of Yahweh's attributes and activity."[21]

All of these proposals are helpful in identifying the transition from despair to hope, and perhaps the variety of suggestions is necessary because not all experiences are the same. Therefore, no single explanation can account for all the changes in moods depicted in these lament psalms. I know from my own experience that when I seek the Lord in my distress, he does not always encourage my heart in the same way. Sometimes I am reminded of his promises in the Bible. Other times he uses circumstances or words of encouragement from other brothers and sisters. Still other

---

[19] Joachim Begrich, "Das priesterliche Heilsorakel," *Zeitschrift für die alttestamentliche Wissenschaft* 52 (1934): 81-92.
[20] John W. M. Wevers, "A Study in the Form Criticism of Individual Complaint Psalms," *Vetus Testamentum* 6, no. 1 (1956): 80-92.
[21] Daniel J. Estes, "The Transformation of Pain into Praise in the Lament Psalms," in Schmutzer and Howard, *Psalms*, 162.

times, he gives me a peace or quiet assurance as I lift up my cares to him. What is important to remember is that lament is a process. The practice of lament is not static; instead, it helps to move us from pain and despair to greater hope and praise. However, this transition is not instantaneous and not always on our timing. Lament is not a quick fix. Sometimes our pain, struggles, shame, or despair can last a lot longer than what we anticipate. This is also reflected in a couple of lament psalms that do not contain this transition to greater hope: Psalm 44 and Psalm 88. As mentioned in chapter 1, the book of Lamentations ends with uncertainty: "unless you have utterly rejected us and are angry with us beyond measure" (Lam 5:22).

Such uncertainty or lack of expression of hope does not mean that the community gave up on Yahweh or that we should do so when we do not experience the comfort or change in circumstances we were hoping for. These dark laments and the abrupt ending in Lamentations leave the outcome open-ended. The psalmist and community were still waiting on the Lord. Sometimes we are called to wait and trust in the mist of our pain and circumstances. This does not mean that all is lost or that we have no hope. In fact, the Hebrew word *qāwāh* ("to wait") can also be translated as hope. Therefore, in our bleakest moments we are called to remember in the darkness what we saw in the light. Let us cling to the Lord in our waiting and say along with Peter, "Lord, to whom shall we go? You have the words of eternal life" (Jn 6:68). Let us continue to turn to him and pour out our pain and requests. Let us press in more closely instead of turning away or hardening our hearts.

In my own darkest moment, I desperately wanted God to come and save the day and bring relief, but the days just kept continuing, and my circumstances remained the same. During that time, all I could do was weep before the Lord and ask him for his comfort. Sometimes even that felt elusive to me, but I kept coming before him. I kept waiting and often crying. I immersed myself in the Psalms and in other parts of Scripture. I clung to his promises. I waited in silence. There were moments when I found great comfort and others when I felt nothing, but this process brought me closer to the Lord. I had never experienced his presence so deeply as I did during those days. He was all I had, and I knew it. I had nowhere else to turn. Waiting on God was humbling and vulnerable, but at the same time, I knew I was waiting on the only one who had the power to help me. These moments tested my faith. If I could not come with faith when I needed him most, when would I truly trust him? God eventually helped me through and brought me to a place that I could not have even imagined for myself, but I look back at those dark times with gratitude. I am thankful that I was not alone and that God heard me. His presence was close even in my deepest pain. He was so faithful.

Vow of praise. This last element is closely associated with the previous one. Because of feeling heard or experiencing deliverance, the psalmist is able to offer a vow or promise of praise (e.g., Ps 13:6; 56:12-13). According to Westermann, this is a frequent component of individual laments and almost always appears at the end of the prayer. However, not all psalms of lament have this component; nevertheless, this last component indicates that God brings hope for a future time. Though lament begins with weeping, God transforms our grief into dancing (e.g., Ps 30:11). Just like the psalmist, when we experience deliverance or assurance, we are to respond with praise.

THE DIFFERENCE BETWEEN CORPORATE (COMMUNAL) LAMENTS AND INDIVIDUAL LAMENTS

While these five essential components are broadly present in the structure of laments in general, there are also specific distinctions that can be made between individual laments and corporate or communal laments. One of the most obvious differences is that corporate laments usually have first-person plural forms, for example *we* or *us*, indicating a collective and not an individual voice. While the exact number of communal laments slightly differ among scholars, Gunkel identifies the following psalms as communal laments: Psalms 44; (58); 74; 79; 80; 83; (106); (125).[22] These prayers usually arose out of crisis situations that the community or nation faced together, for example, military defeat, war, exile, famine, drought,

---

[22]Gunkel, *Introduction to Psalms*, 82. The parentheses indicate the psalm fits into more than one genre type.

corruption in society, and other communal misfortunes. Gunkel also believes these psalms were used during fasting services, which were held by the community in response to general disasters, for example, 2 Chronicles 20:3-5.[23]

Another key distinction in communal laments is that they often appeal to or cite God's earlier saving deeds, for example, Psalms 74:13-17; 80:8-11; 85:1-3. By citing such actions, they are motivating God to intervene as well as praising him for his faithfulness. At times this recollection may even take the place of confession of trust, for example, in Psalm 44:4-8. Additionally, the complaint section in communal laments is more political in nature, often pointing out the ridicule and mockery the psalmists have from their enemies. Lastly, Westermann notes that, in later psalms, the vow of praise or confession of trust may just appear as direct praise of God.[24]

Individual laments, as implied in the title, are oriented toward the individual and feature the usage of first-person singular forms, such as *I* or *me*. The themes and issues raised are general in nature but focused more on individual concerns often evoking great emotion, for example, sickness (Ps 38), internal distress (Ps 42–43), mockery (Ps 22:7), injustice (Ps 69:4-5), personal sin (Ps 51), and enemies (Ps 31:15). Gunkel identifies the following thirty-nine psalms as individual laments: Psalms 3; 5–7; 13; 17; 22; 25–26; 27:7-14; 28; 31; 35; 38–39; 42–43; 51; 54–57; 59; 61; 63–64; 69–71; 86; 88; 102; 109; 120; 130; 140–143. Because there are so many of these, Gunkel characterizes them as the "basic material of the psalter (Book of Psalms)" and adds, "They stand out from other genres by their number alone."[25]

Even though these songs are individual in nature, Gunkel believes that some of them were used during the worship service at the temple in Jerusalem, for example, Psalms 5:8; 28:2. Others had more ordinary contexts, for example, going to bed (Ps 6:6). Unlike communal laments,

---

[23]Gunkel, *Introduction to Psalms*, 82.
[24]Westermann, *Praise and Lament*, 55, 58. In fact, some scholars believe that the vow of praise was only borrowed from individual laments. Most communal laments end with petitions, e.g., Ps 74; 80; 89, or confession of trust/praise, e.g., Ps 44; 84; 89 (Westermann, *Praise and Lament*, 60).
[25]Gunkel, *Introduction to Psalms*, 121-22.

which often focus on political concerns, a number of individual laments speak about threats to life (Ps 22:19-21; 69:2) or death and the underworld (Ps 6:5; 28:1; 88:3-4; 102:11). The imagery in these laments is vivid and moving, but the actual issues are usually expressed in general terms so that it is difficult to determine the specific type of distress the psalmist was experiencing. The psalmist

> reaches for images that powerfully and poignantly reflect his pain and distress, his abandonment, and his betrayal. He appropriates an image as an expression of his feelings to the extent that it appropriately suggests the mood of his spiritual condition. If one image does not suffice, then he multiplies images unconcerned about whether their appearances agree as long as they shock and provoke with their burning colors. In other words, they provide a dynamic impression of what is occurring in his soul.[26]

It is not surprising that, due to their general nature and focus on individual concerns, it is more difficult to assign specific contexts or ceremonies to these prayers. Scholars have also noted that the confession of trust and assurance of being heard is more prominent in these individual psalms than in communal laments. Additionally, unlike communal laments, the vow of praise is a frequent component of individual laments, and it usually occurs at the end of the petition, for example, Psalm 71:14-24.[27]

In the second section of this book, we will look at lament psalms and passages in Scripture that deal with specific situations and struggles. But first we will examine how biblical laments and prayers in the Bible compare with those of Israel's ancient Near Eastern neighbors.

REFLECTION QUESTIONS

1. How does the structure of laments in the Bible inform us about biblical lament? Give specific examples of how these elements go beyond just venting or being sad.

---

[26]Gunkel, *Introduction to Psalms*, 134.
[27]Westermann, *Praise and Lament*, 75.

2. Which of the elements that make up a lament come most easily to you when you are suffering? Which element is difficult for you when you are struggling?
3. How do these elements provide a dynamic rather than a static view on the process of lament?

INDIVIDUAL PRACTICE

Write down the different elements found in biblical laments. Explain each in your own words and give a reason why you think each is important. Try writing a lament for a situation in your own life. Include each of the essential parts. Follow the pattern of the biblical lament, beginning with complaint/petition and ending with confession of trust and vow of praise.

CORPORATE PRACTICE

If you are in a position to have some input into your church's services, incorporate some time in your Sunday worship for corporate lament. This may be simply to pray for the suffering that we hear about in the news or for those who are dealing with difficult circumstances. It may be adding a worship song of lament for those who are suffering or simply giving a moment of silence for congregants to process difficulties they dealt with during the week. If appropriate, also consider designating a time for members in the church to fast together over a situation that the community is facing or that is heavy on the hearts of many in the community.

3

Biblical Lament in the Ancient Near Eastern World

Throughout time, cultures worldwide have practiced lament in various ways. Carleen Mandolfo observes that the two primary forms of lament found across cultures are dirge and "supplication to the deity." As mentioned in chapter two, dirges are associated with death, mourning, and eulogies. While the Bible does have a few examples of this type of lamentation, for example, 2 Samuel 1, the laments we find in the Psalms and other biblical passages fall into the latter category of "supplication to the deity." Mandolfo writes, "In the Psalter, the laments (whether individual or communal) are better understood as crisis language. That is, psalmic laments do not seem to be grieving an irreparable loss so much as appealing to the deity for reparation of status, whether physical, social, or psychological."[1] This type of lament is basically prayer during times of pain and need.

    The Israelites were part of a larger culture in the ancient Near East. Therefore, to gain insight into biblical lament prayers, we must also examine the different neighboring cultures that existed in the ancient Near East. Were laments in the form of supplication to the deity also

---

[1]Carleen Mandolfo, "Language of Lament in the Psalms," in *The Oxford Handbook of the Psalms*, ed. William P. Brown (Oxford: Oxford University Press, 2014), 114.

known in these cultures? What can we learn from these ancient Near Eastern examples? Is there anything particular or different about biblical laments? This chapter will discuss writings from Israel's ancient Near Eastern neighbors and summarize the similarities and differences, especially as they relate to the biblical genre of lament. I will consider the significance of these similarities and differences after comparing writings and prayers from several regions surrounding ancient Israel.

EGYPTIAN

Let us begin our discussion with Egypt. There are only a few hymns and prayers dating from the Old Kingdom (ca. 2680–2160 BC) and Middle Kingdom periods (ca. 2040–1782 BC). The New Kingdom, more specifically the Eighteenth (ca. 1550–1292 BC) and Nineteenth Dynasties (ca. 1292–1189 BC), offers more comparable texts, but even these examples are not like the laments we find in the Bible.[2] The Eighteenth Dynasty prayers are mostly hymns characterized by excessive descriptive praise. There is no lament, petition, or declarative praise (thanksgiving) in these examples. They express praise to god(s) with grandiose compliments related to appearance, attributes, and accomplishments. The Nineteenth Dynasty prayers do exhibit some notable differences from those of the previous dynasty. Texts from Deir el-Medina show that while these later prayers are still hymns of praise, they also contain some petition. Nevertheless, they are still different from the lament prayers found in the Bible. John Walton notes, "Even when petition is present or when a crisis is alluded to, the prayers begin with praise. There is nothing to compare to the lament proper that is found in the individual laments of the Old Testament."[3] Similarly, Othmar Keel points out that rarely did Egyptians come with direct requests to the gods. They usually came with praise and blessing even if petition was the eventual intention. Petitions usually came at the end to explain why all the preceding praise was necessary.[4]

---

[2]John H. Walton, *Ancient Israelite Literature in Its Cultural Context* (Grand Rapids, MI: Zondervan, 1989), 142.
[3]Walton, *Ancient Israelite Literature*, 143.
[4]Othmar Keel, *The Symbolism of the Biblical World* (New York: Seabury, 1978), 313.

In other words, the Egyptians felt the need to soften the hearts of their gods so that they could bring up their petitions. This is not unlike how some kids approach their parents today when they have a request. They usually begin with compliments and sweet praise with the purpose and hope of getting their petitions approved.

As mentioned above, Walton also observes that while Egyptian prayers are full of praise, they do not contain declarative praise or thanksgiving, which is praise to gods for specific individual acts done on behalf of the person praying.[5] However, he is quick to point out that this does not necessarily mean that Egyptians did not offer thanksgiving prayers, only that they were not part of worship in the temple. They could have praised their gods on a more personal level, but if so it was not recorded as part of the official temple worship.[6]

Another notable difference is that Egyptian texts do not really have examples for seeking mercy from gods. Westermann notes, "When the Egyptian psalms speak to the gods there is a preponderance of self-confident assurance, which pushes lament and supplication into the background in favor of a contemplative or pictorial narration that rejoices in the splendor and beauty of the gods. This great self-assurance is striking."[7] If there is sin, the praying persons describe their individual faults as a result of ignorance rather than sin. "In the Egyptian literature there is little disposition to seek divine mercy or to ask for forgiveness since the normal attitude was generally to deny having committed sin altogether."[8] This may seem surprising, but it is better understood in the context of the Egyptian worldview at the time. Egyptian religion emphasized the

---

[5]Walton, *Ancient Israelite Literature*, 145.
[6]Claus Westermann notes another difference between the praise in Egyptian prayer and the praise in biblical laments. He points out that Egyptian descriptive praise, which is praise that focuses on the general attributes and works of the god, usually depicts praise that is in progress or in the indicative form. The Psalms do not describe praise happening; they command it. They usually contain a call to praise. It is something owed to God. "There God is the one who receives and has received praise, while in Israel God is the one whose deeds are an ever new call to praise." Claus Westermann, *Praise and Lament in the Psalms* (Atlanta: John Knox, 1981), 51.
[7]Westermann, *Praise and Lament*, 43.
[8]Edward R. Dalglish, *Psalm Fifty-One: In the Light of Ancient Near Eastern Patternism* (Leiden: Brill, 1962), 95. Daglish does mention that the Book of the Dead and a Theban stela (1350–1200 BC) have examples with petitions for mercy and forgiveness (pp. 96-97).

principle of justice (*ma'at*). This concept held the world together through the belief in act and consequence, also known as the retribution principle. This view basically upholds the expectation that you reap what you sow. If *ma'at* does not operate as it should, then chaos (*isfet*) rules. More specifically, *ma'at* meant "justice" and "cosmic order," as well as "truth and balance."

This understanding was closely tied to Egyptians' view of the afterlife, which thought of the judgment of the dead as the "big" test, when the heart of the dead person was balanced against *ma'at* to determine the fate of the individual. Therefore, for an Egyptian to admit wrong would have upset the balance of the world. To proclaim one's guilt was to admit to the contribution of chaos, which would have detrimental consequences in the afterlife. Example texts from the Egyptian Book of the Dead attest to this kind of thinking. Christopher Hays notes, "Spell 125 of the Book of the Dead is a thoroughgoing denial of wrongdoing—surely the most extensive such denial in the ancient world. It comprises a 'negative confession,' in which the deceased person comes before the tribunal of gods in the Hall of Justice and disavows wrongdoing."[9]

While the concept of *ma'at* contributed to the differences in how the Egyptians approached their gods, there are also some similarities. Bernd Schipper notes that the Great Hymn to Aten discovered in 1884 at Tell el-Amarna is perhaps the only Egyptian text to have a parallel to the Psalms, specifically Psalm 104:20-30.[10] The Hymn to Aten states that the one who guarantees *ma'at* is the sun god, Amun-Re, but on the human level, Pharaoh is seen as the guarantor of justice, and his enemies are seen as representing chaos or *isfet*. The prayer describes the sun god as one

---

[9] However, Hays also mentions that in the Egyptian Book of the Dead the same juxtaposition of approaches to guilt can be seen. "It is less often noted that in Spell 126, which follows directly after the 'negative confession,' the speaker prays to another set of judges ('the baboons who sit in the bow of the bark of Re') to 'expel my evil, grip hold of my falsehood'! So immediately after Spell 125's protestation of purity, the deceased acknowledges that he needs evil and falsehood expunged from him." Christopher B. Hays, *Hidden Riches: A Textbook for the Comparative Study of the Old Testament and the Ancient Near East* (Louisville, KY: Westminster John Knox, 2014), 708.

[10] Bernd U. Schipper, "Egyptian Backgrounds to the Psalms," in Brown, *Oxford Handbook of the Psalms*, 57.

who listens to the prayers of the praying person and conquers enemies by acting as a good shepherd.[11] This role of Amun-Re, although limited because he was one god among many, also reflects the Israelite understanding that one could come to Yahweh for justice. Like Amun-Re, Yahweh is the one who upholds justice in the world. The psalmist can also ask Yahweh to act against their enemies because they are ultimately working against him. Similarly, the Bible also refers to Yahweh as the Good Shepherd and describes his actions in a similar way (Ps 23:5).

This brief description of the differences and similarities in texts from ancient Egypt helps to shed some light on how Israel's neighbor to the south viewed prayer and petition in the light of the Egyptian conception of justice and balance. At the end of this chapter, I will summarize how these differences and similarities compare to Old Testament prayers of lament as well as other ancient Near Eastern examples.

CANAANITE: UGARITIC

There are also not many Canaanite texts that compare with biblical laments. The ones that have been found were from the Hittite Empire in modern-day Turkey and at Ugarit. Discoveries from a Late Bronze Age site of Ugarit in modern-day Syria revealed a great deal of administrative texts and lists. Included also were a few texts that have parallels to parts of the Old Testament, including the Psalms. However, most of these Ugaritic texts were narrative poems, not psalms or prayers. Ultimately there are two notable prayers.[12] In terms of similarities to the Old Testament psalms, they share a particular poetic style with the use of parallelism, which is "a single idea expressed in units of two or three lines by repetition, synonyms, or sometimes antonyms."[13] They also have similar themes, for example, divine kingship, victory over enemies, divine council, and the underworld.

---

[11] See the example of a hymn to Amun-Re that refers to him as the great shepherd in Bernd U. Schipper, "Egyptian Backgrounds to the Psalms," in Brown, *Oxford Handbook of the Psalms*, 60.
[12] For more specifics on the content of these prayers, see Mark S. Smith, "Canaanite Backgrounds to the Psalms," in Brown, *Oxford Handbook of the Psalms*, 44.
[13] Smith, "Canaanite Backgrounds to the Psalms," 45.

A notable difference is that texts dealing with the god Baal give greater emphasis to mythical themes than what we find in the psalms of the Old Testament, although the Old Testament psalms do offer some. Mark Smith observes, "While the Psalms lack the extensive mythological narrative that the Baal Cycle constitutes, they contain mythological allusions to Yahweh's divine enemies, cf. Ps 74:13-14." Smith also argues that some of these Canaanite materials may have served as background for many aspects of the Psalms, but the Psalms indicate developments of these motifs. "First, a psalm may reflect the adaptation of an older Canaanite element. For example, the reference to God in Ps 68:5[4] as one 'who rides upon the clouds' (NRSV, NJPS) is thought to be a direct reflection of Baal's title, 'rider of the clouds.'" He also notes themes in the Ugaritic texts that are not found in the book of Psalms. For instance, the tradition of devotion to the dead prevalent in Ugaritic texts is not present in the Bible. "The psalms represent the Israelite deity as the God of the living and the living God."[14]

John Hastings Patton observes some shared vocabulary between these Canaanite texts and Psalms. "When the vocabulary of the Psalms is compared with all the vocabulary of the Ugaritic literature extant, it is found that approximately 45% of all roots appearing in the Psalms are common to both, while 54% of the roots appearing in Ugaritic are common to both."[15] However, he also highlight that Ugaritic genres are not identical to the biblical ones. Ugaritic texts include poems that are a mixture, containing descriptive praise that blesses the deity, lament, vows, complaint, and petitions for divine help. They are not organized in the same way that we find in the biblical texts. Similarly, William Hallo observes, "Ugaritic texts adduced in all these studies are neither hymns nor prayers and thus can only serve indirectly to illuminate the categories of Biblical psalmody as such."[16]

---

[14]Smith, "Canaanite Backgrounds to the Psalms," 51, 53.
[15]John H. Patton, *Canaanite Parallels in the Book of Psalms* (Baltimore: Johns Hopkins University Press, 1944), 32. In his specific examples he notes distinctive spellings or shortened forms. See 32-45 for more examples.
[16]William W. Hallo, "Individual Prayer in Sumerian: The Continuity of a Tradition," in *Essays in Memory of E. A. Speiser*, ed. William W. Hallo (New Haven, CT: American Oriental Society, 1968), 72.

An obvious difference between Israel's texts and those of all its ancient Near Eastern neighbors, including Ugarit, is the belief in monotheism rather than the polytheism. The Bible is clear that other deities are nothing but idols (Ps 115:4-8). So even though there is shared style, themes, and vocabulary, these texts do not represent approaching the divine in the same manner. As we continue to examine other examples from Canaan and Mesopotamia, we will see how this difference significantly affects the way people prayed and their view of relationship(s) with their god(s).

CANAANITE: HITTITE

There are also not many Hittite parallels to the Old Testament psalms of lament. Earlier Hittite prayers from the Old Kingdom (ca. seventeenth century BC) are more general in nature. They were not written in response to specific events, nor are they linked to specific individuals.[17] Sometime after the beginning of the New Kingdom period (ca. 1450–1200 BC), many royal prayers were written.[18] These prayers name specific kings or royal family members who recited these prayers for themselves or on behalf of their kingdom. They were usually seeking the help of the gods with different problems, for example, enemies, plagues, or illnesses. Like the other ancient Near Eastern neighbors of Israel, the Hittites also worshiped a pantheon of gods. For example, one prayer by Muwattalli II invokes 140 deities of eighty-three different localities.[19] Similar to Egyptian and Ugaritic prayers, Hittite prayers do not have examples of declarative praise (thanksgiving), which thanks the deity for works done on behalf of the individual.[20]

Even though the types of Hittite prayers do not necessarily correspond to biblical laments, nevertheless, there are similarities. For example, some Hittite prayers attest to the deep devotion that the kings and royal family members had toward their gods.[21] This can also be said of the psalmists, though not all the psalmists were of royal descent.

---

[17]Richard H. Beal, "Hittite Prayers," *Journal of Ancient Near Eastern Religions* 4, no. 1 (2004): 155.
[18]P. H. J. Houwink Ten Cate, "Hittite Royal Prayers," *Numen* 16, no. 2 (1969): 81-98.
[19]Beal, "Hittite Prayers," 156.
[20]Hays, *Hidden Riches*, 744.
[21]Giulia Torri, "Strategies for Persuading a Deity in Hittite Prayers and Vows," *Die Welt des Orients* 49 (2019): 49.

One of the most notable differences in Hittite prayers has to do with their transactional view of relationship with their gods. Often the emphasis in these prayers is on "constant transactions between humans and deities: the supplicant is promising something valuable in order to persuade the god to forgive sins."[22] Giulia Torri observes this approach in Mursili II's first plague prayer. She highlights how this prayer promises to reward the sun goddess, Arinna, with bread and libation or drink offerings if she eliminates the plague.[23] While Hays argues that the exact significance of these offerings is not made clear in this prayer, he notes that other Hittite texts describe these offerings as the food of the gods, so perhaps the implication is that the god or gods' very survival is at stake. He points out that only rarely do psalmists suggest that Yahweh should be motivated by sacrifices (e.g., Ps 20:3; 51:18-19; 54:6). In fact, Yahweh's desire for sacrifice is often diminished (Ps 50:12-13; 69:30-31). Instead, the psalmist appeals to Yahweh's desire for praise, as in Psalm 88:10-11. Additionally, Hays suggests that Hittite prayers were quite literally arguments or strategies to persuade the gods. The "Hittite term for a prayer is *arkuwar* and is etymologically related to the English word 'argument.'" He notes, "One of the Hebrew words for prayer, *tephillah*, has similar judicial associations."[24]

While there may be shared terminology between Hittite prayers and the Psalms, the Old Testament in general, including the Psalms, does not display this transactional mindset. It is not a "you scratch my back and I'll scratch yours" approach. In fact, Micah 6:6-8 presents a contrary picture. The Israelites keep asking about and even escalating the type of sacrifices to try to appease Yahweh, but the prophet firmly states that God does not desire sacrifices. Instead, he wants a relationship with his people and for them to walk in righteousness, humility, and justice.

> With what shall I come before the Lord
>   and bow down before the exalted God?
> Shall I come before him with burnt offerings,
>   with calves a year old?

---

[22]Torri, "Strategies for Persuading," 49.
[23]Torri, "Strategies for Persuading," 52.
[24]Hays, *Hidden Riches*, 747.

> Will the LORD be pleased with thousands of rams,
>> with ten thousand rivers of olive oil?
> Shall I offer my firstborn for my transgression,
>> the fruit of my body for the sin of my soul?
> He has shown you, O mortal, what is good.
>> And what does the LORD require of you?
> To act justly and to love mercy
>> and to walk humbly with your God. (Mic 6:6-8)

Yahweh does not respond to his people because they offer sacrifices. Instead, his actions stem from his mercy, lovingkindness, and loyalty to his covenant promises. This is very different from the Hittite mindset. While Hittite prayers touch on similar themes, they are more focused on negotiation with the gods rather than pleading for mercy based on covenantal promises. "Almost all Hittite prayers present a subtle negotiation between human beings and deities, to show that the latter can only reap an advantage by granting the supplicant's request."[25]

Hays also compares Muršili II's first plague prayer with the prayers in the Psalms. More specifically, he compares Muršili II's prayer to Psalms 88–89.

Table 3.1. Muršilli II's First Plague Prayer compared with Psalms 88–89 (excerpted)

Muršili's "First" Plague Prayer to the Assembly of Gods and Goddesses (ca. 1310 BCE)[26]	Psalm 88
§1 (1-7) [All] you male [gods], all female gods [of heaven (?)], all male gods [of the oath], all female gods of the oath, [all] male primeval [gods], all female (primeval) gods, you gods who have been summoned to assembly for bearing witness to the oath on this [matter], mountains, rivers, springs, and underground watercourses. I, Mursili, [great king (?)], your priest, your servant, herewith plead with you. [Listen] to me O gods, my lords, in the matter in which I am making a plea to you! §2 (8-15) O gods, [my] lords! A plague broke out in Hatti, and Hatti has been severely damaged by the plague. And since for	1 LORD, you are the God who saves me; day and night I cry out to you. 2 May my prayer come before you; turn your ear to my cry. 3 I am overwhelmed with troubles and my life draws near to death. 4 I am counted among those who go down to the pit; I am like one without strength. 5 I am set apart with the dead, like the slain who lie in the grave, whom you remember

---

[25]Torri, "Strategies for Persuading," 59.
[26]Itamar Singer, *Hittite Prayers* (Atlanta: Society of Biblical Literature, 2002), 61-64. Singer notes that this prayer by Muršilli is addressed to the entire pantheon of gods. There are two extant exemplars of the text, a single-column tablet and a late double-column copy.

twenty years now in Hatti people have been dying, the affair of Tudhaliya the Younger, son of Tudhaliya, started to weigh on [me].
§3 (16–22)
[But when my father] wronged Tudhaliya, all [the princes, the noblemen], the commanders of the thousands, and the officers of Hatti [went over] to my father. The deities by whom the oath was sworn [seized] Tudhaliya and they killed [Tudhaliya].
§4 (23–40)
But now you, O gods, [my lords], have eventually taken vengeance on my father for this affair of Tudhaliya the Younger. My father [died (?)] because of the blood of Tudhaliya, and the princes, the noblemen, the commanders of the thousands, and the officers who went over [to my father], they also died because of [that] affair.
§7 (13′–20′)
Now, because Hatti has been severely oppressed by the plague, and the population of Hatti continues to die, the affair of Tudhaliya has troubled the land. It has been confirmed for me by [the god], and I have further investigated [it] by oracle. They are performing before you, [O gods], my lords, the ritual of the oath which was confirmed for you, [O gods], my lords, and for your temples, with regard to the plague of the land and they are clearing [it (i.e., the oath obligation) before] you. And I am making restitution to you, O gods, my lords, with reparation and a propitiatory gift on behalf of the land.
§8 (21′–40′)
Because you, O gods, my lords, [have] taken vengeance for the blood of Tudhaliya, those who killed Tudhaliya [have made] restitution for the blood. But this bloodshed is finished in Hatti again: Hatti too has already made restitution for it. Since it has now come upon me as well, I will also make restitution for it from my household, with restitution and a propitiatory gift. So may the soul of the gods, my lords, again be appeased. May the gods, my lords, again be well disposed toward me, and let me elicit your pity. May you listen to me, to what I plead before you. I have [not] done any evil. Of those who sinned and did the evil, no one of that day is still here. They have already died off. But because the affair of my father has come upon me, I am giving you, O gods, my lords, a propitiatory gift on account of the plague of the land, and I am making restitution. I am making restitution to you with a propitiatory gift and reparation. May you gods, my lords, again [have] mercy on me, and let me elicit your pity. Because Hatti has been oppressed by the plague, it has been reduced in size. [And those makers of offering bread and libation pourers who used to prepare] the offering bread and the libation for the gods, my lords, [since Hatti] has been severely oppressed by [the plague], [they have died] from the plague. [If the plague] does not subside at all, and they continue to die, [even those] few [makers of offering bread] and libation pourers [who still remain will die, and nobody will prepare] for you offering bread and libation any longer.

no more, who are cut off from your care.
6 You have put me in the lowest pit, in the darkest depths.
7 Your wrath lies heavily on me; you have overwhelmed me with all your waves.
8 You have taken from me my closest friends and have made me repulsive to them.
I am confined and cannot escape;
9 my eyes are dim with grief.
I call to you, Lord, every day; I spread out my hands to you.
10 Do you show your wonders to the dead? Do their spirits rise up and praise you?
11 Is your love declared in the grave, your faithfulness in Destruction?
12 Are your wonders known in the place of darkness, or your righteous deeds in the land of oblivion?
13 But I cry to you for help, Lord; in the morning my prayer comes before you.

Psalm 89
1 I will sing of the Lord's great love forever; with my mouth I will make your faithfulness known through all generations.
2 I will declare that your love stands firm forever, that you have established your faithfulness in heaven itself.
3 You said, "I have made a covenant with my chosen one, I have sworn to David my servant,
4 'I will establish your line forever and make your throne firm through all generations.'"
5 The heavens praise your wonders, Lord, your faithfulness too, in the assembly of the holy ones.
17 For you are their glory and strength, and by your favor you exalt our horn.
18 Indeed, our shield belongs to the Lord, our king to the Holy One of Israel.

§9 (41'–51') May [you gods, my lords], have mercy on [me again] because of the offering bread and the libation which [they prepare for you], and let me elicit your pity. Send the plague [away from Hatti]. Let those few makers of offering bread [and pourers of libation] who [still remain] with you not be harmed, and let them not go on dying. Let them prepare [the offering bread] and the libation for you. O gods, my lords, turn the plague [away, and send] whatever is evil to the enemy land. Whatever has happened in Hatti because of Tudhaliya, send it [away] O gods, [my lords]. Send [it] to the enemy land. May you again have mercy on Hatti, and let [the plague] subside. Furthermore, [because] I, your priest, your servant, elicit your pity, may you have mercy on me. Send away the worry from my heart, take away the anguish from my soul!	**26** He will call out to me, "You are my Father, my God, the Rock my Savior." **27** And I will appoint him to be my firstborn, the most exalted of the kings of the earth. **28** I will maintain my love to him forever, and my covenant with him will never fail. **29** I will establish his line forever, his throne as long as the heavens endure. **30** "If his sons forsake my law and do not follow my statutes, **31** if they violate my decrees and fail to keep my commands, **32** I will punish their sin with the rod, their iniquity with flogging; **33** but I will not take my love from him, nor will I ever betray my faithfulness. **34** I will not violate my covenant or alter what my lips have uttered. **35** Once for all, I have sworn by my holiness—and I will not lie to David— **36** that his line will continue forever and his throne endure before me like the sun; **37** it will be established forever like the moon, the faithful witness in the sky." **38** But you have rejected, you have spurned, you have been very angry with your anointed one. **39** You have renounced the covenant with your servant and have defiled his crown in the dust. **40** You have broken through all his walls and reduced his strongholds to ruins. **41** All who pass by have plundered him; he has become the scorn of his neighbors. **42** You have exalted the right hand of his foes; you have made all his enemies rejoice. **43** Indeed, you have turned back the edge of his sword and have not supported him in battle.

	44 You have put an end to his splendor and cast his throne to the ground. **45** You have cut short the days of his youth; you have covered him with a mantle of shame. **46** How long, Lord? Will you hide yourself forever? How long will your wrath burn like fire? **47** Remember how fleeting is my life. For what futility you have created all humanity! **48** Who can live and not see death, or who can escape the power of the grave? **49** Lord, where is your former great love, which in your faithfulness you swore to David? **50** Remember, Lord, how your servant has been mocked, how I bear in my heart the taunts of all the nations, **51** the taunts with which your enemies, Lord, have mocked, with which they have mocked every step of your anointed one. **52** Praise be to the Lord forever! Amen and Amen.

In terms of similarities, both the Hittite prayer and psalms remain "in darkness, in lament, to their very end. . . . These prayers leave their speakers still waiting for divine intervention."[27] However, Psalm 88 is more individual in nature, seemingly referring to personal suffering and death, compared to the Hittite prayer, where the king is speaking on behalf of the nation and even functions like a chief priest. According to Hays, Hittite prayers usually contain both hymnic material and requests for help; but this plague prayer has almost no praise. There are also shared themes in these prayers. For example, Psalm 89 remembers Yahweh's past protection in the same way the Hittite prayer refers to the past positive state. Similarly, Hays notes that both the Hittite prayer and Psalm 89 have a strong royal character.

---

[27] Hays, *Hidden Riches*, 744.

In terms of differences, the Hittite prayer tries to distance the present generation from the previous one in order to absolve their guilt. For example, Mursili attributes his people's suffering to the vow his father broke. While his father did perform a ritual to clear his own guilt, the nation of Hatti remains guilty because they did not perform any rituals on their own behalf. Because of this, Mursili states that he is making restitution on behalf of the land, but he also makes it clear that he has not done any evil. Moreover, of those who did sin, no one from that day remains. This is contrary to Psalm 89, which emphasizes the connection to past generations. There is no distancing from Israel's forefathers.[28] Last, unlike the Hittite prayer, Psalms 88–89 do not identify the reason for divine wrath.[29] Hays thinks this points to the fact that the reasons for the suffering have "recede(d) from importance in the mind of the speaker. The cry is loud and clear: Make it stop."[30] In other words, the psalmist is not focused on retribution but imploring for Yahweh to bring relief.

While Canaanite examples from Ugarit and the Hittite Empire have some similar themes, poetic form, and vocabulary in comparison to biblical lament, there are many underlying differences in these ancient cultures' approach to their gods. Let us now turn to the prayers found in Mesopotamia.

MESOPOTAMIAN

Among all the ancient Near Eastern neighbors of Israel, Mesopotamia, which includes Sumer and Babylonia, has the largest collection of prayers that could be compared to biblical laments. In the earlier periods of Mesopotamia, written prayers to the gods were often inscribed on votive objects that were placed in temples near the statute of the deity whom they addressed. These objects included bowls, weapons, or statues of the person asking favor from the gods. In many instances, they were "considered as taking the place of the supplicant and relieving him of the need

---

[28]Hays, *Hidden Riches*, 746-47.
[29]There are other psalms that do confess guilt, e.g., Ps 51.
[30]Hays, *Hidden Riches*, 750.

to proffer his prayer in his own person, orally and perpetually."[31] As time progressed, this method became too costly, so written prayers or letters to the deity were left at the temple instead.[32] These prayers along with others were discovered in Sumer and Babylonia.

John Walton lists the following categories and examples of Mesopotamian prayers that have been found:

Table 3.2. Categories and examples of Mesopotamian prayers

Prayer to *Ishtar*—Tentatively dated to the middle of the second millennium. Written in Akkadian.
Eršemma (Wail of the Shem-drum)—Two different types were found. The first were Old Babylonian versions that were narratives based on mythological motifs. The later versions were psalms used to appease their gods and were also considered incantations. These were composed in the *Emesal* dialect of the Sumerians, which was a dialect used in literary texts and recited by *gala* priests who served in the temples.
Eršaḫunga (Lament to Calm the Heart)—Individual laments used to address sorrow or hardships (usually not sickness) caused by the gods rather than enemies. Twenty-six examples written in the *Emesal* dialect were found. These also included Akkadian translations.
Šuilla (Raising of the Hand)—Both Sumerian and Akkadian examples were found. Forty-seven were Sumerian and composed in the *Emesal* dialect. They don't necessarily contain lament proper sections and were not considered incantations. There was also 150 Akkadian *Šuillas*, some are only fragments or duplicates. These were prayers also considered incantations or enchantments to be spoken, sung, or performed along with ceremonial rituals.
Ki-ᵈUTU-kam/ *Ki'utukam* (Incantation of Utu/Shamash)—These were Sumerian and Akkadian[33] incantations to the rising sun and used for purifying sin, uncleanness, or illness.
Dingir.ša.dib.ba (Incantation for Appeasing an Angry God)—Very similar to the *Šuilla* and *Eršaḫunga*, but these may have been a subcategory of other genres. There were seven examples of this found. Later ones in late Assyrian and late Babylonian were also identified.
Šurpu ("Burning")—This is a series of prayers and incantations that included magical rites. Seven tablets with prayers addressed primarily to Marduk were found. The burning refers to a rite of purification and is used when the person praying is unsure of the sin or offence that he/she had committed. There are also other examples that have prayers to the gods, which were also associated with incantations or rituals for averting evil.

Source: John H. Walton, *Ancient Israelite Literature in Its Cultural Context* (Grand Rapids, MI: Zondervan, 1989), 137-40.

---

[31] Hallo, "Individual Prayer in Sumerian," 75.
[32] For specific examples of these letters, see Patrick D. Miller, *They Cried to the Lord: The Form and Theology of Biblical Prayer* (Minneapolis: Fortress, 1994), 10-13.
[33] Patrick D. Miller, *They Cried to the Lord: The Form and Theology of Biblical Prayer* (Minneapolis: Fortress, 1994), 14.

In addition to these example, Patrick Miller lists two additional types of texts:

Table 3.3. Additional categories and examples of Mesopotamian prayers

Aḫulap—An Akkadian term that has been translated as "it is enough." It signifies a general cry for help and represented a general form of prayer for help.
Šigû—An Akkadian term that implies a plea for pardon and came to designate a particular type of penintential prayer.

Source: Patrick D. Miller, *They Cried to the Lord: The Form and Theology of Biblical Prayer* (Minneapolis: Fortress, 1994), 7.

Jessica McMillan compared the Sumerian Prayer of Lamentation to Ishtar with biblical laments and notes various similarities and differences.[34] First, this poem has similar elements to biblical laments: invocation, praise to the deity, complaint, and petition. Similar phrases are also used, for example "How long?" and "seven times seven."[35] There are also some stylistic similarities, such as the usage of poetic devices and allusions to certain themes, for example, destruction, illness, request for deliverance, and sacrifices. Like Egyptian prayers, the Sumerian Lamentation to Ishtar contains extensive praise at the beginning of the prayer. McMillan cites these initial praises from the prayer (10:1-6):

> Text to be recited: Ishtar of the stars, goddess of the morning!
> Lady of ladies, most high of goddesses!
> Bright one of the Igigŭ, light of the lands!
> Most high of gods, lightening (. . .)
> Brilliant star, bright torch, who (in the distance)
> Becomes bright, you lighten the mo[untains!][36]

As noted above, this extensive praise at the beginning of a prayer is not found in biblical laments. McMillan observes, "In Israel, lamenters did not attempt to flatter their deity as the Mesopotamians did. Most biblical

---

[34] Jessica McMillan, "A Comparison of Ancient Near Eastern Lament to Selected Passages of Biblical Lament," *Artistic Theologian* 9 (2021): 161-78.
[35] McMillan, "Comparison of Ancient Near Eastern Lament," 167.
[36] Anna Elise Zernecke, "Mesopotamian Parallels to the Psalms," in Brown, *Oxford Handbook of the Psalms*, 30.

laments begin with a brief invocation such as 'Oh Yahweh' or 'My God.' This insinuates that Yahweh can be approached with confidence and without pretense. While Mesopotamian laments typically begin with praise, biblical laments typically end with praise."[37] Similarly, Westermann comments on the praise present in Babylonian psalms. The difference in the praise "lies in the fact that in Babylonian psalm the emphasis lies entirely on the praise which prepares the way for the petition, and in the Psalms of the O.T. it lies entirely on the praise that looks back on the wonderful help of God in intervening."[38] However, Westermann does point out that both Babylonian and biblical psalms include a vow of praise as an essential component, and it usually comes after the petition, toward the end of the poem.

Walton also observes that, like Egyptians and Canaanite prayers, Babylonian prayers also do not praise their gods for specific individual acts done on behalf of the individual.[39] Similarly, Westermann detects,

> In Babylon the psalms primarily praise the one who exists, the god who exists in his world of gods. In Israel they primarily praise the God who acts marvelously by intervening in the history of his people and in the history of the individual member of his people. The gods praised in Babylon have their history among the gods. In Israel's praise from beginning to end the basic theme is the history of God with his people.[40]

Another point of difference, raised by Anna Elise Zernecke, is that the Prayer to Ishtar begins the lament with an introduction of the person praying. "'I am N.N., son of N.N., whose god is *Marduk*, whose goddess is *Zarpanitu*' (Ishtar 10:43-35). As a typical element in Akkadian prayers, the self-introduction could be adapted for various persons in different

---

[37]McMillan, "Comparison of Ancient Near Eastern Lament," 168. Zernecke notes that there are a few Mesopotamian prayers that have no hymnic introduction, like the biblical laments ("Mesopotamian Parallels to the Psalms"). However, these are only prayers directed to personal protective gods of the person praying (*Dingir.ša.dib.ba* prayers). These were prayed to minor gods, unlike Ishtar, a high god.

[38]Westermann, *Praise and Lament*, 42.

[39]Walton, *Ancient Israelite Literature*, 145. Again, this does not mean Babylonians did not pray in this way. It just was not part of worship in the temple. It may have taken place on a more personal level, not part of official corporate praise.

[40]Westermann, *Praise and Lament*, 42.

situations by naming the supplicant in the execution of the ritual. It has, however, no direct parallel in the biblical psalms."[41]

This type of introduction is also seen in *šuilla* ("raising of the hand") prayers and contains ritual accompaniment along with the introduction by a ritual expert. Zernecke suggests that this process mirrored that of coming before a ruler who was seated in his court.[42] These *šuilla* prayers, as well as prayers to higher gods, like the one to Ishtar, reflect a distance between the human person and the gods. This distance is not present in the biblical psalms, which speak of Yahweh as a refuge and shield.

Another aspect that should be acknowledged is that just as those who approached a human ruler would not come empty-handed, similarly, many Sumerian and Babylonian prayers were also accompanied by rituals, such as sacrifices or gifts, to appease the gods so that the requests would be granted. These rituals or gifts were given to motivate the deity to grant the praying person's request. This desire to engage, motivate, or even pacify the gods was also a common concern in *Dingir. ša.dib.ba* prayers, which were penitential prayers that served as incantations for appeasing angry gods. An important aspect of these penitential prayers was that they tried to identify and confess sin to appease an angry deity. "The petitioner comes in penitence seeking reconciliation and release of sin and its consequences from the deity, who is angered because of some action by the praying one that is not specified in the prayer."[43]

Because these prayers were incantations, ritual action was emphasized through specific directions. Some prayers that have been found are accompanied by directions, which include the use of amulets, the placing of blood on houses, or even burning items to dispel the evil that was thought to be causing the supplicant's suffering.[44] As Hays writes, "Mesopotamian prayer texts have been preserved with rubrics, that is,

---

[41] Zernecke, "Mesopotamian Parallels to the Psalms," 30. The N.N. refers to a wildcard where the supplicant would insert his own name and family heritage. Zernecke also notes in note 14 that in a different text of this prayer, there are also wildcard characters for the names of the deities as well (37). Perhaps this type of introduction indicates that this was a typical or formulaic way of approaching the gods and goddesses.

[42] Zernecke, "Mesopotamian Parallels to the Psalms," 33.

[43] Miller, *They Cried to the Lord*, 20-21.

[44] Miller, *They Cried to the Lord*, 22.

ritual instructions. . . . Tablets read, for example, 'You recite this [incantation] three times and it will be released,' or 'He shall stand facing the ritual paraphernalia of a man's god and goddess and he shall recite [the prayer].'"[45] Biblical psalms are not incantations and do not have explicit directions for ritual actions accompanying them.[46] Some psalms actually downplay the use of ritual sacrifices and offerings to appease Yahweh. Psalm 51:16-17 says,

> You do not delight in sacrifice, or I would bring it;
> > you do not take pleasure in burnt offerings.
> My sacrifice, O God, is a broken spirit;
> > a broken and contrite heart
> > you, God, will not despise.

However, there are other psalms that speak about freewill offerings given to the Lord (Ps 54:6) and vows accompanied by thank offerings (Ps 56:12; 61:8). The role of sacrifices in Israel seems to have been different from those in Mesopotamia. Similar to other ancient Near Eastern cultures, Mesopotamian prayers also reflect a transactional view of relationship between human beings and the divine.

Like in Egypt, Mesopotamian prayers also take a stance of ignorance regarding sin. However, the reason is different from Egyptian prayers. Instead of fearing judgment or contribution to chaos, Mesopotamians pleaded ignorance because they did not really know what they may have done to offend the different gods. Miller writes, "Particular attention should be called to the claim of ignorance. The claim not to know the sin that has been committed is ubiquitous in the prayers. The system of omens did not always undercover the particular sin that was regarded as evoking divine wrath."[47] Again, this is different from biblical psalms, which acknowledge either guilt or innocence. Perhaps the claim of ignorance is not present because Israel's religion was not polytheistic. When there were so many gods, it was hard to keep track of sins that could have angered the different gods.

---

[45]Hays, *Hidden Riches*, 699.
[46]Hays, *Hidden Riches*, 699.
[47]Miller, *They Cried to the Lord*, 18.

Another difference in the Mesopotamian prayers, again stemming from Mesopotamians' polytheistic worldview, is the belief that one god could intercede for the petitioner to other gods. Miller says, "Not infrequently a suffering person will pray to his or her personal god to intervene in his or her behalf to one of the high gods," or even vice versa.[48] In the polytheistic system, a hierarchy existed among the gods. Individuals did not have personal relationships with the high gods but had personal gods who were thought to be able to advocate on their behalf. The polytheistic system denied total sovereignty to any individual god; however, it is interesting that the higher-level gods are often praised as if they were totally sovereign.

While such a petition for intercession is generally not categorized as incantation, some scholars regard it as falling under the category of magic. According to Leo Oppenheim, "The supplicant turns to the specific intercession deities presumably because they provide in some magical way an immediate contact with the great gods whose reactions then affect the personal protective gods either directly or through some message or command."[49] Miller writes of Egyptians that they "also approached the deity through intermediaries, but it was often tied to statues and images of the deified king or important office bearers that were erected in the temple precincts. These figures were to be the messengers bearing the prayers to the god."[50]

As we have seen, Mesopotamian examples are probably the closest in form to the Old Testament psalms. Nevertheless, they also contain differences as a result of the mindset of their neighbors in the ancient Near East. Before discussing the significance of the similarities and differences mentioned in this chapter, I will present one last category of Mesopotamian prayers. These are communal prayers that are closely related to Lamentations, which was written in the context of the destruction of Jerusalem by the Babylonians.

---

[48] Miller, *They Cried to the Lord*, 22.
[49] A. Leo Oppenheim, "Analysis of an Assyrian Ritual (Kar 139)," *History of Religions* 5, no. 2 (Winter 1966): 263.
[50] Miller, *They Cried to the Lord*, 23.

SUMERIAN CITY LAMENTS

Many of the prayers discussed above are considered individual prayers, although in some cases the king or the royal figure is praying on behalf of the nation using first-person plural forms. But there also exist examples of a separate type or genre called city laments. These prayers mourn the fall of cities and reflect on the significance these events. Even though these laments are different from the communal lament genre in the Psalms, they can inform our understanding of Lamentations. The following five Sumerian city laments from Mesopotamia are extant: a lament for Ur, a lament for Sumer and Ur, a lament for Nippur, a lament for Uruk, and a lament for Eridu.

These laments were written in response to the destruction of Sumerian cities at the end of the Ur III period (end of the twenty-first century BC) and the early Isin period (twentieth century BC).[51] The city-states involved include Ur, Nippur, Eridu, Akkad, and Lagash. Like other Sumerian laments, these were mostly written in the Emesal dialect. The content and form of these texts varies, but they have shared themes. All of them speak of the destruction of the city and its temple as a result of famine, military attacks, plague, or drought (or multiple of these disasters combined). They also speak of the loss of inhabitants, the decision of the gods to destroy the city, and abandonment by the city's protector god, as well as the restoration of the city and temple and the return of the protector god. Hays observes that these laments close with a prayer to the deity "involving either praise, plea, imprecation against the enemy, self-abasement, or a combination of these elements."[52]

Later forms, called *balags* and *ershammas*, are derived from the city laments. These newer forms began to appear around the same time that the older city laments disappeared (in the Old Babylonian period, ca. 2000–1500 BC). The *balags* and *ershammas* "were used when a sanctuary was to be razed and restored (the restoration and remodeling of temples was a major pastime of ancient Near Eastern rulers), but also during the *akitu*

---

[51]Hays, *Hidden Riches*, 780.
[52]Hays, *Hidden Riches*, 780.

festivals."⁵³ Unlike their predecessors, these newer forms are more general in nature and could be adapted for various cities and contexts. The *ershammas* are compact and "addressed to a single deity." *Balags* are "more general in description of disaster and could be borrowed from city to city."⁵⁴ Hays suggests that they were composed at the time of the city's destruction or when the events were fresh in the minds of survivors. The content was then adapted to be used in various temple services.

While there are shared themes between these city laments, in both their older and newer forms, and Lamentations, Walton argues that "the theological function ... of Lamentations has no parallel in Mesopotamian literature."⁵⁵ Similarly, Thomas McDaniel writes that parallels to the Sumerian city laments are only superficial and that "there is no need to assume here that the Hebrew poet of Lamentations drew from outside his own covenant traditions when he wrote of divine purpose."⁵⁶ Conversely, W. C. Gwaltney argues that while the theological function is different, there are similarities that show that Israel could have borrowed from the later *balags* and *ershammas* in the composition of Lamentations. "Because of the polytheistic theology underlying the Mesopotamian laments and their ritual observance, they could not be taken over without modification in theology and language. Still the biblical book of Lamentations was more closely associated with the Near Eastern lament genre than simply borrowing the idea of a lament over the destruction of a city."⁵⁷ F. W. Dobbs-Allsopp also argues that even though there are no exact parallels between the Mesopotamian laments, other features, such as the theme of divine abandonment or divine agent of destruction may point to the process of adaptation and there could be some similarities between the genres.⁵⁸

---

⁵³Hays, *Hidden Riches*, 781.
⁵⁴W. C. Gwaltney Jr., "The Biblical Book of Lamentations in the Context of Near Eastern Lament Literature," in *Scripture in Context II: More Essays on the Comparative Method*, ed. William W. Hallo, James C. Moyer, and Leo G. Perdue (Winona Lake, IN: Eisenbrauns, 1983), 197-98.
⁵⁵Walton, *Ancient Israelite Literature*, 163.
⁵⁶Thomas F. McDaniel, *The Alleged Sumerian Influence upon Lamentations* (Leiden: Brill, 1968), 205.
⁵⁷Gwaltney, "Biblical Book of Lamentations," 211.
⁵⁸F. W. Dobbs-Allsopp, *Weep, O Daughter of Zion: A Study of the City-Lament Genre in the Hebrew Bible* (Rome: Gregorian & Biblical Press, 1993), 126-27.

I include this comparison between the book of Lamentations and Sumerian city laments to show that literature does not arise out of a vacuum. Contextual influences and previous prototypes can be used to shape later works. Previous themes or genres can also be adapted to fit a particular culture or situation. However, these later works do not have to mirror the theological or philosophical understandings of previous works. Although similarities exist, the differences can be instructive and illuminating.

LEARNING FROM SIMILARITIES AND DIFFERENCES

So, what can we learn from examining the prayers of Israel's neighbors? How does this help us as we desire to recover biblical lament? How does lament in the Old Testament reflect the culture of its time, and how does it differ? More importantly, what can we infer and learn from these differences?

While Israel's ancient Near Eastern neighbors offered prayers to their gods during difficult times, many of the texts that have been discovered do not fully correspond with laments in the Old Testament. Nevertheless, many of these texts and prayers do have similar elements, vocabulary, and themes. All of the examples we examined reflect the belief that the god(s) uphold justice and bring vindication, healing, and relief. This similarity in themes suggests a shared view in the ancient Near East about the existence of divine beings and their ability to help people. The worldview of ancient Near Eastern people went beyond the physical world. They believed that they could appeal for divine assistance when difficulties arose, such as during times of famine, sickness, enemies, and pestilence. They also saw divine beings as greater in ability than humans. Therefore, it is not surprising that gods are praised extensively for their character and general deeds displayed in creating and sustaining the world. It is also not surprising that people appealed to the gods for help, whether in bringing relief or in intercession with other deities.

While Israel's ancient Near Eastern neighbors shared a similar understanding of the interaction between the physical and spiritual world, there are some foundational theological differences from Israel reflected in their prayers. These differences can be summed up in the following two perspectives: (1) how ancient Near Eastern people viewed the relationship between human beings and the divine, and (2) how their prayers functioned.

The relationship between human beings and the divine. One fundamental theological difference between Israel and its neighbors concerned the type of relationship human beings could have with their god(s). Inevitably, this understanding was also shaped by belief in polytheism versus monotheism. A polytheistic worldview made it difficult to have personal interactions with all the gods. This understanding is reflected in several differences that appear in prayers. The first is ignorance of sin, especially in the Mesopotamian prayers. Israel's neighbors had to be mindful of the pantheon of gods that existed, and it was difficult to keep track of the ways they could have provoked or displeased different gods. Oftentimes even omens could not uncover what wrongs people had committed against the gods. Moreover, what was considered offensive to one god may not have been to another. Second, intercession from other gods on behalf of the praying person was thought to help secure favor with other gods in the context of the hierarchy that existed. It was not enough to be in harmony with one's personal god; one needed help from other gods to ensure one's overall well-being. The sheer number of gods and the complexity related to this system contributed to the sense of distance when approaching the divine.

Thus, when people came before a high god, such as Ishtar, they needed to introduce themselves and come with gifts or offerings. They also began their interactions with extensive praise to ensure a positive response from the deity. In other words, they had to put their best foot forward so that the gods would be willing to hear and answer their requests. Prayers do not reflect an intimate relationship. Perhaps this also contributed to people's proclamation of innocence. They did not want the gods to think that they had any part in contributing to chaos (*isfet*). They also felt the need to distance themselves from the sins of their forefathers to dispel any doubt about their innocence. These steps were taken to help ensure that they would receive a positive outcome from the gods they were praying to.

Another difference, also reflecting a more distant relationship with the divine, is the lack of declarative praise or thanksgiving for specifics acts that the gods performed on behalf of the individual. Even the most elaborate praise is for general attributes and general actions of the god(s) in the world. We do not see any personal thanksgiving on behalf of the individual praying. Prayers also emphasized the mythical elements of gods, implying a greater chasm between the divine and human worlds.

This perspective is very different from what we find in the Bible. To begin with, the Old Testament does not present a polytheistic worldview. Yahweh is the only God. He is the Creator and the sustainer of the world. He is not unfamiliar with those who come in prayer before him. The prayers in the Psalms do not reflect a God who is removed and distant. Instead, the psalmist speaks of his relationship with God in intimate terms. For example, in Psalm 27:10 the psalmist declares with confidence that even if his own parents abandoned him, he knows that Lord would still take care of him. This confidence and intimacy are very different from Israel's neighbors, who had to formally introduce themselves before different gods, especially those higher up in the hierarchy. No formal introduction is needed when approaching Yahweh. In fact, he knows the psalmist intimately, even before he was born (Ps 139:16). While the psalmist at times complains about God's silence or distance, it is always predicated on the fact that this is outside the norm. Biblical laments display the intimacy Yahweh had with his people.

Israel also had a special covenant relationship with Yahweh.[59] Because of this, the psalmist can come in his presence without any pretense. This is evidenced in that the praying person does not have to praise God extensively before pouring out his heart. A simple call or invocation to Yahweh can lead straight into lament, complaint, or requests. Moreover, the psalmist does not need another god to intercede on his behalf. The

---

[59]To be sure, this covenant relationship also comes with covenant obligations, which the Old Testament prophets continued to proclaim, e.g., Hos 4. These prayers and the confidence that the psalmists had in approaching God do not minimize their covenant obligations. While this is not the focus of my book, it is important to note that covenant obligations were central for the Israelites (see Exodus, Leviticus, Deuteronomy, and the books of the prophets). The exile was a consequence for their failure to fulfill these obligations (see Deut 29:22-28).

psalmist can come into God's presence without having to secure favor through a third party. One does not have to come without sin or on one's best behavior. Instead, the psalmists often express their pain or distress without reservation and freely admit guilt as well as innocence. They also do not have to distance themselves from their forefathers to absolve guilt, but often identify with the sins of their forebearers (Ps 106:6).

While many of the psalms in the Old Testament are related to royalty, especially King David, a feature they share with a number of other ancient Near Eastern texts, many others are anonymous. This anonymity makes these psalms even more relatable, freeing us to pray these same prayers today. Bruce Waltke notes that most of the psalms have both royal and messianic significance in the context of their use during the First Temple, but with the advent of Jesus, the context has changed. "We conclude then, that the Psalms are ultimately the prayers of Jesus Christ, Son of God. . . . Moreover, Christians, as sons of God and as royal priests, can rightly pray these prayers along with their representative Head."[60] Therefore, it is important to remember that these prayers are not to be limited in application to only a particular group of ancient Israelites. They have contemporary relevance even for us as New Testament believers through the work and life of Jesus.

The differences we have discussed are important not only because they highlight the uniqueness of our relationship with God, but because they demonstrate the intimacy we can have with him. As New Testament believers, we can experience even greater communion as his people because we have the Holy Spirit living in us (2 Cor 6:16). This should encourage us to come before God with confidence. We do not have to put our best foot forward. What Christ has done on the cross has given us access to the throne room of grace (Heb 10:19). This understanding is foundational when we think about recovering biblical lament that is rooted in the laments found in Scripture. We can only truly lament if we can come without pretense, knowing that our God hears and knows us intimately. We do not have to let shame or doubt hold us back.

---

[60] Bruce K. Waltke and Fred G. Zaspel, *How to Read and Understand the Psalms* (Wheaton, IL: Crossway, 2023), 538.

We can also offer thanksgiving instead of just general descriptive praise because Yahweh is a personal God who answers the prayers of his people. The Old Testament constantly speaks of God hearing the cries of his people and delivering them (Ex 3:7-8). In fact, declarative praise (thanksgiving) psalms are usually associated with individual laments because they were prayed in response to God's answers. Westermann writes, "Here it becomes clear that (declarative) praise results from God's action. God's intervention is the source of declarative praise."[61] Again, that declarative praise exists in the Bible is a testimony that prayers of lament do not go unheard. We are not praying to a God whom we hope will hear. No, we are praying to Yahweh, our Heavenly Father. Not only is he able to answer, but he does answer. He cares for us and desires the very best for our lives. And we are not alone in our suffering, as Jesus also intercedes for us. Romans 8:32-34 reminds us,

> He who did not spare his own Son, but gave him up for us all—how will he not also, along with him, graciously give us all things? Who will bring any charge against those whom God has chosen? It is God who justifies. Who then is the one who condemns? No one. Christ Jesus who died—more than that, who was raised to life—is at the right hand of God and is also interceding for us.

That the book of Psalms has declarative praise (thanksgiving) reminds us that God sees us in our times of need and in our pain. As he answered the psalmists, he will answer us. We are not just casting prayers into the abyss of the spiritual realm without any assurance of being heard. Our prayers are not just wishful thinking or conscious manifestations that we put forth into the universe. No, they are our heartfelt cries and truthful desires expressed before a personal God who cares for us.

How prayers function. The other difference between Israel and its ancient Near Eastern neighbors is how they viewed the function of prayer. As noted above, many ancient Near Eastern prayers were transactional. For example, the Hittites provide reasons or arguments for why the gods should be persuaded to forgive sins or eliminate suffering. Such reasons

---

[61] Westermann, *Praise and Lament*, 102.

are often related to or accompanied by sacrifices and offerings that the petitioner is bringing or pledges to bring. While some similar terminology may exist in the Psalms, the Old Testament is clear that Yahweh regards righteousness and justice as more important than sacrifices. "To do what is right and just is more acceptable to the LORD than sacrifice" (Prov 21:3). In other words, Yahweh is not persuaded to act by mere sacrifices and offerings.

Additionally, many Sumerian and Babylonian prayers also fall under the category of incantations that included rituals requiring gifts or sacrifices to appease the gods. These rituals were performed to attempt to ensure a positive outcome. That many of these rituals also include recited incantations reinforces the transactional mindset. Having a step-by-step process probably felt easier and safer when approaching the divine than coming in total surrender and vulnerability. Their emphasis is not on asking for mercy or forgiveness. Responses were thought to be dependent on performing the correct rituals and bringing the right offerings. This understanding is different from the laments found in the Old Testament. While the psalmist does offer vows of praise (Ps 22:22; 71:18), these do not function as incantations. Earlier Babylonian and Egyptian prayers also had vows of praise in addition to sacrifices.[62] But as Westermann points out, in the Old Testament "the vow of praise has not simply taken the place of one of the sacrifice(s).... Praise is not a substitute for sacrifice." Vows were not offered to try to ensure a positive outcome. Instead, they were part of the transition from lament and petition to praise. "That lamentation and petition can change into praise in the same psalm has a consequence, a development which is peculiar to the Israelite psalms, that is, that praise is already heard in the conclusion of lament and petition, and this forms the basis for the vow of praise."[63]

This distinction is important when we think about recovering biblical lament because it reinforces that biblical lament is a process. It is not a

---

[62]"The vow of praise lost its importance and finally disappeared entirely. It was no longer regarded as necessary. This can be seen in the Babylonian prayer literature and even more clearly in that of Egypt.... This process can also be observed in the petitionary Psalms of the O.T." (Westermann, *Praise and Lament*, 78).

[63]Westermann, *Praise and Lament*, 77-79.

formula or incantation. When we lament before God, we are waiting on him. As we pour out our pain, disappointment, shame, and suffering, we are not engaging in a transactional ritual. We are coming before Yahweh, who is our Heavenly Father. We are sharing our deepest thoughts, desires, and hopes. Through this process the psalmist often finds a new outlook and a new expectation that leads to greater hope. Just as Job and Habakkuk are given a new perspective through their encounter with God, many psalms of lament also exhibit this change. There is transformation in God's presence through the process of lament. As mentioned in chapter three, a progression from despair to hope is displayed in many psalms of lament. Biblical lament prayers are not bargaining or manipulating God into action; instead, they are engaging God in full surrender and vulnerability. Like the apostle Paul, in lament we can experience God's strength in our weakness (2 Cor 12:9-10).

This brief survey on the prayers of Israel's ancient Near Eastern neighbors points to the importance of recognizing the differences between the Israelite perspective and those of their surrounding context. Recovering biblical lament rooted in the genre of biblical lament is to remember that our prayers are directed to Yahweh, who is not only omnipotent but knows us deeply. We do not have to introduce ourselves or offer extensive praise for him to hear our requests. We do not have to bargain or offer gifts for a positive response. Instead, we can be honest and vulnerable with him because of the relationship we have through Jesus. Our prayers are not transactional. Instead, they reinforce the relationship we already have with God. Through prayer we are humbling ourselves before God, asking for his mercy and help, asking him to right wrongs, asking for healing and justice. We are entering into deeper communion with him. Most importantly, we are waiting on his timing and trusting in his goodness and justice. Recovering biblical lament is ultimately living into the relationship we have with the Lord in our time of need.

REFLECTION QUESTIONS

1. How do the prayers of Israel's neighbors help us to see the unique nature of biblical lament?

2. What are some general theological differences between the Old Testament's view of deity versus that of its neighbors? How did these differences affect prayers in different cultures?
3. While Israel shared a similar understanding of the interaction between the physical and spiritual world with its ancient Near Eastern neighbors, there were some foundational theological differences.
    a. What were the specific differences? Which one stood out to you the most?
    b. How do these differences help you to appreciate biblical lament?

INDIVIDUAL PRACTICE

Take some time now to reflect on how you approach God in your prayers, especially when you are going through difficulties. Are you coming before God trying to bargain with him to take away your pain? Do you see your relationship with him as transactional? Are you trying to be on your best behavior so that he will listen and answer you? If so, spend some time meditating on how God is your Heavenly Father and how he is not out to crush you or see you suffer. If necessary, spend time repenting for the wrong perspectives you may have about him. Ask God to give you the correct perspective about him and about your suffering. Ask him for the patience to wait on his timing and his will. As your meditation and reflection leads, allow yourself to surrender your will, give praise, or lift up further petition.

CORPORATE PRACTICE

Does a transactional mindset prevail in your church? Consider discussing this topic in your small group(s). Small group leaders can provide space for members to share about their personal challenges in prayer during times of suffering, then pray together for each member.

4

The Purpose of Lament

Whether we are currently experiencing pain or witnessing others go through it, we recognize that life is far from perfect. Dark times are inevitable and often lurking around the corner. If we live long enough, we all face suffering in one form or another.

Our own lives mirror the story of Scripture, which quickly unfolds as a story that moves through moments of deep grief and loss with hope. Genesis attributes this broken state to the fall of humanity, depicted in Genesis 3. Through the events that transpired in the Garden of Eden, our world became subject to sin and along with it suffering and alienation. Not only did humankind incur the judgments pronounced there by God, but we now experience shame, fear, and loneliness. We know that Jesus' work on the cross has provided us hope beyond the grave, but now we experience life with God in an imperfect world that is full of sin and suffering. If we are honest, sometimes the future hope of our faith does not bring us the comfort we so desperately desire when we are going through suffering. We read Scripture and know that joy comes in the morning, but that does not make the ache of our souls dissipate. Whether shame from pain we have caused others or suffering we experience because of some external wrong thrusted on us without our consent, these feelings of sadness, grief, and guilt can often linger with no foreseeable end. This is where lament comes in. Lament helps us to engage with God now, as we await our future hope.

Practically speaking, lament is a multifaceted means God has graciously provided to help us process the brokenness and fallen state of the world that we reside in, whether experienced through pain, loss, suffering, sickness, sin, or injustice. Lament has various functions that move us toward healing and wholeness. This chapter will focus specifically on the purposes of lament in the following three general categories: to give voice to our pain, to provide an avenue to engage God, and ultimately to lead us into greater hope.

TO GIVE VOICE TO A PERSON IN PAIN

Lament enables us to process our suffering. One of the primary ways this is accomplished is through acknowledgment, because we cannot deal with what we do not acknowledge. Throughout the Old Testament and especially in the Psalms, we observe raw expressions of pain, disappointment, confusion, doubt, hatred, and even anger. There is no fronting or faking here. Scripture shows us that only when we are honest can we deal with the issues that are burdening us. Too many of us would rather sweep things under the rug or keep ourselves busy so we do not have to face the ugliness that arises in our hearts. We are quick to tell people that we are fine when we really are not. Perhaps we do not want to confront our issues because it is too painful, or perhaps we fear judgment from others or think it is unspiritual to let others see our struggles.

When I was teaching a seminary course in Hong Kong on this topic, some of the church leaders who attended the class confided that they would not let their church members see them struggle because they feared being judged. Some of them had actually experienced judgment and were ostracized for being honest. Unfortunately, they are not alone, and this is not limited to churches overseas.

Many pastors also perpetuate the idea that it is inappropriate to be friends with congregation members, which contributes to the internal divide they experience between what they portray to others and their true selves. For some reason, Christians have equated spirituality with always being happy, in control, or fine. I have often heard people say, "I don't want to go to church today because I am not feeling up to it." Do we think that we must be in a certain positive or capable state to be able to go to church? Do we believe that being happy and content honors God more?

The Purpose of Lament

Or perhaps we are reacting the way Adam and Eve did when they hid from God because they felt ashamed. When we read the Bible, we find that we are in the company of friends when we suffer. Mary the mother of Jesus has to watch her own son die. Joseph is sold into slavery by his own brothers. Job experiences tremendous loss and physical suffering. Elijah suffers from depression and loneliness, and the apostle Paul experiences both inner and outer turmoil because of his ministry. Let us remember that God does not expect us to come to him as perfected people who are competent and qualified; he wants to meet us in our struggle and pain. Matthew 11:28 says, "Come to me, all you who are weary and burdened, and I will give you rest."

Ironically, when we silence our pain and doubts, we weaken rather than strengthen our faith. Faith is not displayed in the soul that does not struggle. Biblical faith is one that is strengthened more through trials than through well-being. Suffering is often a process of refinement that purifies us and brings to the surface our true emotions, sins, fears, and doubts. Instead of suppressing or covering these emotions, we need to learn to be honest. We must be people who are willing to say that we are not okay and live authentically before God, ourselves, and others. We must be willing to grieve our losses and pain openly. This is very biblical. We see in Acts 8:2 that "devout men buried Stephen and made great lamentation over him" (ESV). Paul and his companions also express deep sorrow over the prospect of never being together again in Acts 20:38: "What grieved them most was his statement that they would never see his face again." When we acknowledge our pain, even if it is temporary, we create space for God and others to enter into healing with us. I will speak about this a little more later in this chapter.

Perhaps another reason we do not give voice to our pain is that we would rather numb our feelings because the pain is too great. Avoidance through busyness or other distractions is easier to handle. For some of us, our busyness has become a badge of honor, and we just do not have time to deal with "emotional, touchy-feely stuff." Or we think it is just easier to ignore our feelings because facing them requires too much energy. But ignoring our struggles through busyness or other distractions does not make them go away; in fact, often it worsens the situation. Instead of experiencing healing and peace, we find ourselves more easily agitated. One study found that bottling up emotions can make people more aggressive.[1] The study asked one groups of participants to suppress their emotions when watching notoriously disturbing scenes from several movies, while another group was able to express their emotions. Those who suppressed their emotions were more aggressive afterward than subjects who were allowed to show their feelings. On this topic, clinical psychologist Victoria Tarratt says,

> For example, you might be angry at your brother and after stewing in your anger, not saying a thing, you could encourage an emotional outburst. So when you're driving the car a few weeks later and someone cuts you off, you can get all-out road rage, causing an accident. That explosion and overreaction to a situation is your body's way of releasing that pent-up emotion.[2]

Similarly, Kathleen O'Connor observes,

> The first condition for healing is to bring the pain and suffering into view. Only then can they be examined, allowed, and given their due. Demand their due they will; they will neither diminish nor disappear until they are met face to face. Pain kept from speech, pushed underground and denied, will turn and twist and tunnel like a ferret until it grows in those lightless spaces into a violent, unrecognizable monster.[3]

If we suppress or ignore our emotions, we may temporarily experience some reprieve, but these latent feelings will rear their ugly heads when we are least expecting it. Part of giving voice to our suffering is giving ourselves the permission to feel. However, we tend to struggle with doing this for various reasons. Perhaps we grew up in a home that

---

[1] K. D. Vohs, B. D. Glass, W. T. Maddox, and A. B. Markman, "Ego Depletion Is Not Just Fatigue: Evidence from a Total Sleep Deprivation Experiment," *Social Psychological and Personality Science* 2, no. 2 (2011): 166-73.
[2] Lucy Cousins, "Can Always Staying Positive Be Bad for Our Health?," HCF, updated August 2022, www.hcf.com.au/health-agenda/body-mind/mental-health/downsides-to-always-being-positive.
[3] Kathleen O'Connor, *Lamentations and the Tears of the World* (Maryknoll, NY: Orbis Books, 2004), 103.

preached the "suck it up and walk it off" philosophy. This mentality applauds a stoic disposition that makes us seem impervious to pain. We can start believing that nothing will affect us if we suppress negative emotions. But this is a grave misunderstanding of human nature. God did not create us to be robots; he made us human being with emotions and feelings. And our emotions are interconnected with other areas of life. Other studies have shown that when we suppress our emotions, they present themselves in other ways, for example, physical ailments. One study found a strong correlation between emotional suppression and cancer onset and progression.[4] Additional studies also found that emotional suppression can lead to heightened physiological reactivity, which also makes people more vulnerable to disease.[5] A 2013 study showed people who bottled up their emotions increased their chance of premature death from all causes by more than 30 percent, with their risk of being diagnosed with cancer increasing by 70 percent.[6] Conversely, James W. Pennebaker found that "confronting our deepest thoughts and feelings can have remarkable short- and long-term health benefits."[7] We are not just rational, physical, or emotional beings; we are whole persons. If we do not deal with our feelings, they will come out in other ways.

Therefore, it should not shock us that the Bible is full of support for a full expression of our emotions, affirming much of what the latest psychological research is saying. We do not have to carry these burdens alone. The psalm writers have provided us examples for processing our doubts,

---

[4]J. Gross, "Emotional Expression in Cancer Onset and Progression," *Social Science & Medicine* 28, no. 12 (1989): 1239-48; see also Gabor Maté, *When the Body Says No: The Cost of Hidden Stress* (New York: Knopf, 2003).

[5]D. S. Krantz and S. B. Manuck, "Acute Psychophysiologic Reactivity and Risk of Cardiovascular Disease: A Review and Methodologic Critique," *Psychological Bulletin* 96, no. 3 (1984): 435-64; J. M. MacDougall, T. M. Dembroski, and D. S. Krantz, "Effects of Types of Challenge on Pressor and Heart Rate Responses in Type A and B Women," *Psychophysiology* 18, no. 1 (January 1981): 1-9; Andrew Steptoe, "Psychological Factors in Cardiovascular Disorders," *Journal of Psychosomatic Research* 26, no. 6 (January 1982): 636.

[6]Benjamin P. Chapman, Kevin Fiscella, Ichiro Kawachi, Paul Duberstein, and Peter Muennig, "Emotion Suppression and Mortality Risk over a 12-Year Follow-Up," *Journal of Psychosomatic Research* 75, no. 4 (October 2014): 381-85.

[7]James W. Pennebaker, *Opening Up: The Healing Power of Expressing Emotions* (New York: Guilford Publications, 2012), 2.

pain, shame, grief, anger, and struggles. When we practice lament and face our issues with honesty before the Lord, we are allowing God to speak into these situations. We are no longer sitting in the echo chambers of our own minds; instead, we are allowing the Lord to speak into the depths of our hearts. This is similar to the first steps toward physical healing. If we never address our physical health issues, we will not find the remedies we need. The first step is to go to a physician for an examination. We must expose ourselves and our pains to the doctor. This is not an easy process, and it can often be painful if we have left our wounds festering for some time. However, once we reveal our troubles, we are one step closer to healing because the doctor can now prescribe the necessary treatment. We need to apply this course of action to our emotional and spiritual life as well. God is our Great Physician. When we come before him with full disclosure and honesty, no matter how ugly it is, we are expressing our desire for healing and wholeness.[8]

In her seminal work on trauma, Judith Hermann writes that avoiding traumatic memories leads to stagnation in the recovery process.[9] It is not a coincidence that cognitive psychotherapy has linked healing from trauma with oral and written narrative retelling. June Dickie indicates that cognitive therapists help patients reconstruct their trauma memory through retelling, whether through written or verbal means, and then remove the associated negative emotions while integrating it into the patient's personal biography.[10] This process often takes old traumatic memories and images and associates them with new, positive images so that the original memories are not activated. This helps the trauma victim to reclaim their narrative, thus giving them a voice. Instead of keeping the memories buried and subconsciously wreaking havoc, the victim can face the pain, grieve, and move toward transformation. Martin Symonds writes, "Creating the trauma account . . . reduces the sense of isolation,

---

[8] This process may also require us to be open and honest with others, including mental health professionals.
[9] Judith Lewis Herman, *Trauma and Recovery: The Aftermath of Violence—from Domestic Abuse to Political Terror* (New York: Basic Books, 2015), 176.
[10] June F. Dickie, "The Intersection of Biblical Lament and Psychotherapy in the Healing of Trauma Memories," *Old Testament Essays* 32, no. 3 (2019): 889.

providing opportunity to be heard by someone."[11] Lament is a way for us to give voice to our pain. Burying our feelings stunts our growth. When we give voice to these emotions through lament before God, we can move toward healing and wholeness.

This process also allows us to regain control or agency. Viewed in this way, lament is also an act of resistance. When we are suffering, we often feel powerless and voiceless, but through lament we are reclaiming our emotions rather than giving our pain and suffering the final word. Hermann observed in her work with trauma victims, "Reclaiming the ability to feel the full range of emotions, including grief, must be understood as an act of resistance rather than submission to the perpetrator's intent." She found that when victims of trauma, whether from abuse or other forms of violence, were able to lament and feel their emotions, they were able to move forward, even without closure from their perpetrators. She notes, "As grieving progresses, the patient comes to envision a more social, general and abstract process of restitution, which permits her to pursue her just claims without ceding any power over her present life to the perpetrator. . . . This restitution in no way exonerates the perpetrator of his crimes, rather, it reaffirms the survivor's claim to moral choice in the present."[12] Instead of staying stuck in the cycles of self-harm, resentment, shame, and depression, survivors are able heal and make progress.

TO GIVE VOICE TO A PEOPLE IN PAIN

Individual lament is important, but corporate lament also plays a role in the healing process. Lament is not just for individuals who are walking through pain and crisis; it is also for the communities around such people. In this way, lament helps communities to understand those who are in pain and to stand alongside them. Even if we have not been touched by the situation, we can acknowledge and see those who are in pain. Pain can be isolating for those who are enduring it, so when a community laments

---

[11] Martin Symonds, "Victim Responses to Terror," *Annals of the New York Academy of Sciences* 347 (1980): 129-36.
[12] Herman, *Trauma and Recovery*, 188, 190, 193.

with the individual, they are standing in solidarity with and offering comfort to the sufferer. In Lamentations 1, suffering Lady Zion calls out for someone to witness her pain (Lam 1:12). Additionally, the refrain "there is no comforter" is repeated four times in this first chapter (Lam 1:2, 9, 17, 21), further depicting the isolation Lady Zion is feeling. As we recognize the suffering of others, it broadens our perspective of the world. O'Connor states, "The voices of Lamentations urge the readers to face suffering, to speak of it, to be dangerous proclaimers of the truths that nations, families, and individuals prefer to repress. They invite us to honor the pain muffled in our hearts, overlooked in our society, and crying for our attention in other parts of the world."[13] Corporate lament reminds us that we live in a world full of suffering, but we are not alone. There will also be times when we suffer collectively. Henri Nouwen calls us to live in community and with compassion in the context of suffering. "Community and solidarity are at the heart of the movement from sorrow to joy. When you begin to feel the pain of your life in relation to other people's pain, you can face it together. This is where the word compassion comes from (com-passion = passion, to suffer with)."[14]

I participated in a lament service held by a Christian institution that had experienced a great deal of pain due to mistrust, divisions, and decisions that some saw as insensitive. The morale of many dissipated into cynicism and apathy. As new leadership took the helm, they wanted to hold a lament service to acknowledge the pain so that healing could begin and greater hope could be restored. The service gave time for mourning as well as acknowledgment of the hurt that many had experienced. It also allowed time for prayer as a corporate body to lament the loss and to pray for unity. Many who attended felt encouraged. Some shared that it was healing for them to be able to participate in this type of service and that they felt seen and heard by the community. This time of lament brought closure to a difficult season and united the community in ways that promoted greater hope going forward.

---

[13]O'Connor, *Lamentations and the Tears*, 102.
[14]Henri Nouwen, *Spiritual Formation: Following the Movements of the Spirit* (New York: HarperOne, 2010), 75.

There are also times when corporate lament protests the injustices experienced by the sufferer. In these cases, lament is a prophetic act that gives voice to pain. Again, Scripture gives testimony to this. Prophets in the Old Testament often call out specific injustices and ignite imagination for what the community could be if it stood for true justice and mercy.

In these cases, lament is the appropriate response to horrors that have taken place. Communities that stand as a witness for those who are suffering exercise a love that is other-centered. This decentering not only helps us to hear the sufferer but also provides an opportunity for the community to speak truth against the injustices and evils that may have caused the suffering. Instead of normalizing systemic injustice by turning a blind eye, acknowledging it through lament helps the community to amplify the voices of those who are suffering. However, acknowledgment alone is not the end; this act of communal lament is also an invitation to make a change. Lamenting as a community functions not only to call out evil by speaking truth but also to collectively advocate for those who are suffering. And this opens the way toward healing. N. T. Wright speaks of the Commission for Truth and Reconciliation in South Africa, which formed in the aftermath of apartheid:

> Though most Western journalists have taken little notice of it, the fact of white security forces and black guerillas both confessing in public to their violent crimes is itself an awesome phenomenon. And with those confessions, the families of tortured and murdered have been able for the first time to begin the process of true grieving, and thereby at least to contemplate the possibility of being able to forgive, and so pick up the threads of their lives instead of being themselves overwhelmed and continuing anger and hatred.[15]

Relatedly, Henri Nouwen writes, "I realized that healing begins with taking your pain out of its diabolic isolation and seeing that whatever we suffer, we suffer in communion with all of humanity, and, yes, all of creation. In so doing, we become participants in the great battle against the powers of darkness. Our little lives participate in something much larger

---

[15] N. T. Wright, *Evil and the Justice of God* (Downers Grove, IL: InterVarsity Press, 2006), 134.

and universal."[16] Lament is a language for pain that gives voice to suffering. Individuals and communities must stand together in lament to acknowledge the brokenness in our world so we can take steps toward healing and change.

TO PROVIDE AN AVENUE TO ENGAGE GOD

When we practice lament, we are not just giving voice to our suffering; we also are bringing it before God. Sorrow, anger, and other emotions often cause us to retreat rather than to engage with others. Sometimes this can be very subtle. For example, while scrolling on our phones or watching Netflix can for a time be an acceptable way to cope with overwhelming emotions, it does not lead to comprehensive healing. As discussed previously, lament creates an avenue for feelings of suffering, pain, and anger to have a voice. Conversely, isolating coping strategies often result in apathy or even numbness. When this happens, we are not only not giving voice to our pain, but we are shutting down communication in the context of our relationships. One study found that suppression of emotion closes down relationships and further disengages the individual. People who suppress their emotions often avoid close relationships. The study found that "over time, the cumulative effect of avoiding closeness would likely be an impoverished social network and the erosion of the individual's social support, particularly in terms of its socioemotional aspects."[17] But emotional suppression does not only affect our relationship with people; it affects our relationship with God. This is why biblical lament is important and why we have so many examples of laments in Psalms. The psalmists are not afraid to cry out to God with raw emotion.

Often, we let only those who are closest to us see our pain and real self—warts and all. If God is truly our closest friend and Heavenly Father, why do we try to hide from him? He already knows us better than we know ourselves. In response, some would argue that, if God knows us so

---

[16]Nouwen, *Spiritual Formation*, 76.
[17]James J. Gross and Oliver P. John, "Individual Differences in Two Emotion Regulation Processes: Implications for Affect, Relationships, and Well-Being," *Journal of Personality and Social Psychology* 85, no. 2 (2003): 356.

well, why do we need to lament? Again, this is a misunderstanding of lament. Lament is more than just pouring out our feelings and emotions before God; it is an act of faith because we are turning to him instead of away from him. Lament means that we are not alienating ourselves from God, which we often tend to do in difficult times. It is not a coincidence that so many Christians stop reading the Bible, praying, going to church, and interacting with Christian friends when they are suffering, shutting off various avenues that might lead to connection with God. Instead of choosing to come before God and receive comfort from him, we would rather suppress our feelings, or worse, turn away from God altogether. Sadly, many times our instinctual response is probably closer to Job's wife's advice to "curse God and die" (Job 2:9). Through the act of lament, we invite God into our struggles, whether in grief, pain, anger, depression, sin, or doubt. This is exactly what we see in Job's response to his suffering. Instead of heeding his wife's advice, he brings his issues before God in raw honesty and vulnerability.

Lament also helps us to recognize that we are not alone in our struggle. Jesus is appropriately called Immanuel, "God with us." A vivid example of this in Scripture is when Jesus appears to the two disciples on the road to Emmaus. As the resurrected Christ, he asks them a question he should know the answer to, "What are you discussing together as you walk along?" (Lk 24:17), and asks for further details in Luke 24:19. He sees that they are downcast and asks them to share their thoughts with him. In other words, he invites their laments. He then listens patiently as they express their disappointment and doubts (Lk 24:19-24). He spends time explaining to them the Scriptures concerning himself (Lk 24:27). He does not chastise them for not recognizing him or for their failure to understand. When the disciples finally recognize Jesus, they recall that that their hearts burned within them when Jesus spoke the Scripture to them (Lk 24:32). This is a story of Jesus lovingly walking with disciples who are downcast and disillusioned. Their hopes have been dashed, and their desires seem unfulfilled. Jesus knows this but invites them to share and patiently listens and responds to them. He does not expect them to snap out of it. He also does not say, "Don't worry about it because God is working out everything for the good of those who love him." Instead, he asks them to tell him about their pain and discouragement. Although the disciples do not recognize him at the outset, Jesus listens to their story and helps them to process their disappointments and doubts. God similarly invites us into his presence to lay our burdens down, where he can meet us in our pain. The practice of lament makes room for relationship, for telling our story, for making ourselves vulnerable.

Hebrews 4:15-16 tells us that we can approach the throne and ask God for help in our time of need because we have a high priest who can empathize with our weaknesses. This applies not only to our supplication but also to our laments. When we are vulnerable before God, we are in essence turning to him for help. He will not reproach us; instead, he will show mercy and grace to help us in our time of need (Heb 4:16). This enables us, as sinners, to approach God as we are. We do not have to put on any masks or pretend. We can come before him with our weaknesses and pour our needs before his throne. Jesus our high priest, who has been tempted in every way, understands us. We have this reassurance, and we are given the invitation to come before God. We do not have to carry our burdens alone, and we do not have to be afraid to engage God even though we are sinful human beings. Unlike Adam and Eve, who retreated in guilt and shame, we can come boldly before God's presence in faith, seeking to engage and commune with him.

Lament also enables us to be in a true covenant relationship with God. Instead of coming to God only with our praises, we can also express our feelings of discouragement, doubt, anger, confusion, and pain. Too often we think that we can approach God only with thanksgiving. To be sure, thanksgiving and praise are important in our interactions with God, but these are not the only ways for us to engage God in faith. When we bring only our praises and thanksgiving before God, we are showing merely a part of our true feelings. We are not really interacting with God in a genuine way. Walter Brueggemann explains,

> One loss that results from the absence of lament is the loss of genuine covenant interaction because the second party to the covenant

(the petitioner) has become voiceless or has a voice that is permitted to speak only praise and doxology. Where lament is absent, covenant comes into being only as a celebration of joy and well-being. Or in political categories, the greater party is surrounded by subjects who are always "yes men and women" from whom "never is heard a discouraging word." Since such a celebrative, consenting silence does not square with reality, covenant minus lament is finally a practice of denial, cover-up and pretense, which sanctions social control.[18]

When we lament, we are engaging in faith with God in true relationship. This is the only way to foster true intimacy. We clearly see this in our human relationships. Think about how you put on a front of positivity to impress people whom you do not know well, which commonly occurs on social media. When you do so, you present a curated version of yourself. In our intimate relationships, when we are healthy we often show frustration, grief, disappointment, and hurt as well as hope and joy.

Lament is an act of faith because we are approaching God with the belief that he can make a difference in the situations we are facing. We are not just pouring out emotions; we are seeking change. This is clear in the psalms of lament. As Craig Broyles writes, "Lament psalms invite the worshiper to vent their frustrations and pour out their feelings, but there comes a time to seek a way out. . . . These psalms seek change, and they are based ultimately on promise, not doubt. They acknowledge that something is wrong and affirm that God can put it right."[19] We are acting in faith when we lament because we are not giving discouragement, doubt, anger, or pain the last word. We are expressing these emotions before God, who not only walks with us through the process but can make things right. This aspect of lament is predicated on the fact that God is one who is powerful, loving, and just. Because he is who he is, we can approach him in this way.

---

[18]Walter Brueggemann, "The Costly Loss of Lament," *Journal for the Study of the Old Testament* 36 (1986): 60.

[19]Craig Broyles, "Lament, Psalms of," in *Dictionary of the Old Testament: Wisdom, Poetry and Writings*, ed. Tremper Longman III and Peter Enns (Downers Grove, IL: InterVarsity Press, 2010), 396.

This aspect of faith expressed through lament is especially highlighted in situations of evil and injustice. In such contexts, we are trying to reconcile events and actions in this unjust world with God's character. Biblical lament trusts God enough to cry out. Sometimes lament is the only and most appropriate response to the horrors that take place because some evils are so appalling that only the infinite goodness and power of God can bring about their ultimate defeat. The cry of lament is a cry for change. It is naming the evil and pain that has befallen us and our world.

When we engage God in the context of evil, we can also experience a deep communion that participates in his ultimate plan. We can pray along with the Lord's Prayer that "your kingdom come, your will be done, on earth as it is in heaven" (Mt 6:10). As Brueggemann says, we are not just "yes men and women," and our prayer life should be one that reflects faith that God can do mighty things. When we engage in lament, we are asking God to right the wrongs, not only in our individual lives but in our world. This is exemplified in the prayer of the prophet Habakkuk.[20] He brings before God the injustices that he sees and asks God to take action (Hab 1).

Seen in this way, lament can also enrich our prayer lives. Too many of us are content with trite and shallow prayers. We offer thanksgiving and lift up some requests, but are we truly engaging God in faith? Are we being honest? How do our prayers sound? Are they vague and unfocused? Are we just praying generally for others and for the world? Are we constantly at a loss for words? Perhaps we do not truly believe that God can make a difference. When we pray, we need to remember that we are coming not only to our Heavenly Father but to the God of the universe. James 4:8 tells us that when we draw near to God, he will draw near to us. Are we willing to do the hard work of reconciling the pains, doubt, depression, and anger that reside in our hearts with the faith we have in our great God? Or are we content to numb our emotions, which leads to disconnection from God, because they seem too overwhelming?

---

[20]While the individual prayers of lament in Habakkuk do not contain all the elements of the lament genre, they are present in all three prayers together. There are three prayers in Habakkuk 1: prayer 1 in Hab 1:2-4 (address, lament/complaint), prayer 2 in Hab 1:17 (motivations), prayer 3 in Hab 3:1-19 (confession of trust and vow of praise).

The Purpose of Lament

The Bible gives us plenty of examples of true engagement with God through lament. Let us learn and join with them in faith, with fervent and honest prayers.

TO LEAD US INTO GREATER HOPE

The goal of lament is not to wallow in our pain. This is another misunderstanding people can have. It can seem that lament is not necessary because it leads only to navel-gazing and ultimately stagnation in faith. On the contrary, the purpose of lament is to lead us into greater hope. As we lament, we are putting ourselves in a posture of waiting and anticipating God's response and work. Claus Westermann notes, "There is not a single psalm of lament that stops with lamentations. Lamentation has no meaning in and of itself. . . . What the lament is concerned with is not a description of one's own sufferings or with self-pity, but with the removal of the suffering itself. The lament appeals to the one who can remove suffering."[21]

All too often the things that cause us pain and grief are things we cannot bring to a resolution by our own strength. Suffering can stem from the evil actions of others, our own sins, death, physical illness, injustice, or other things that are out of our control. This is exactly why we need to come before the Lord in lamentation. Psalm 126:4-6 exemplifies this well. These verses are a cry of lament for God to restore the fortunes of those praying. In the historical context of the exile and postexilic period, the Hebrew word translated as "our fortunes" (*šəbûtēnû*) can also be understood as referring to the desire to be free from captivity or imprisonment. This is why some versions translate it "restore our captivity," for example, Amplified Bible and KJV, or even "restore our captives," for example, NAB. The psalmist is lamenting and asking God to act on behalf of his people. They are in a situation where they cannot restore themselves. They need God to step in. It is important to note here that while Psalm 126:4 is the cry for help, Psalm 126:5-6 speaks of the subsequent joy that will result. "Those who sow with tears will reap with songs of joy. Those who go out weeping,

---

[21]Claus Westermann, "The Role of the Lament in the Theology of the Old Testament," *Interpretation* 28, no. 1 (1974): 26.

carrying seed to sow, will return with songs of joy, carrying sheaves with them." Our tears of lament are seeds that will blossom into joy. In other words, our suffering and discouragement will result in greater joy.

Sometimes the road through the valley of lament is what brings true praise. This begs the question of what is true praise. Does this mean that all our suffering will go away and we receive everything we asked for? Not necessarily, in fact, many who have lamented speak more about their deep intimacy with God than the deliverance they experienced. It is not surprising that I have heard countless testimonies from those who have suffered deeply that they found their deepest joy during these times of suffering. For most, these were the moments they felt closest to the Lord. A student in my class shared of an illness that resulted in isolation due to the pain and embarrassing symptoms that accompanied this illness. She spent many months alone with God. As she shared her journey, she spoke of the deep joy she found in the Lord through this experience. God's presence became real, and with it came an intimacy and joy that filled her heart. What brought her true praise was the ability to walk with God and know him more intimately, rather than the eventual healing that she experienced.

Lament is based on God's promises and his character, not in hopelessness. We can lament because of who God is and his promises. He is a good and just God who is merciful and compassionate. He is mighty to save and able to deliver his people. It is precisely because he is just, faithful, and compassionate that we can pray and call him to act accordingly. Our salvation is not based on our own righteousness. The prophet Daniel knew this well as he lamented the state of Jerusalem during the exile. "Give ear, our God, and hear; open your eyes and see the desolation of the city that bears your Name. We do not make requests of you because we are righteous, but because of your great mercy" (Dan 9:18).

The process of lament provides us the space to reconcile what we know about God and his promises with what we are experiencing. We can question and grapple with the incongruencies and lift them up before the Lord. This is evident in Habakkuk. The prophet questions God based on his character: "Your eyes are too pure to look on evil; you cannot tolerate wrongdoing. Why then do you tolerate the treacherous? Why are you silent while the wicked swallow up those more righteous than themselves?" (Hab 1:13). Lament is the space we need to move from our doubts, pains, and anger to a place of worship. Habakkuk models this well because it starts out in Habakkuk 1 with the prophet's doubts and questions and ends in Habakkuk 3 with a beautiful psalm of worship and praise. Even though the prophet does not witness the resolution that he hopes for, he is still able to hope and wait on the Lord. Lament provides a path through suffering, which leads to greater hope and even praise in the midst of difficult circumstances.

God does not expect us to snap out of our emotions. Other people may expect that, and sometimes we expect it from ourselves, but our emotions are more complex. We cannot generally will ourselves out of depression, anger, or grief. It is usually a process we need to walk through to find true healing and growth. I once heard a sermon from Joseph Stowell in which he warned, "One of the worst things you can do as a Christian is to go around with this plasticized mask on saying, 'I love God and he's so good,' when your heart is breaking inside." Sadly, this is all too common because we think this is how we count it all joy when we are going through trials (Jas 1:2). The movement from lament to praise is not always on our timing. Sometimes it takes the hard work of processing our doubt, anger, and pain, but when we are able move into a place of praise, we realize that the process of lament actually helped to enhance our praise and worship of God. Westermann writes,

> Just as lamentation is the language of suffering, so the praise of God is the language of joy. One is as much a part of man's being as the other. But it is an illusion to suppose that there could be a relationship with God in which there was only praise and never lamentation. Just as joy and sorrow in alternation are a part of the finitude of human existence, so praise and lamentation are part of man's relationship to God. Hence, something is amiss if praise of God has a place in Christian worship, but lamentation does not. Praise can retain its authenticity and naturalness only in polarity with lamentation.[22]

---

[22] Westermann, "Role of the Lament," 27.

The structure of Psalms also captures this movement well. Westermann points out that there are more laments at the beginning of the book and more psalms of praise toward the end of the collection.[23]

As we lament all the pain, suffering, and injustice we see, we are also able to focus on who God is as well as remembering what God has done in the past. Reciting what God has done is a common theme in lament as a genre, especially communal laments. Through this process of reflection and remembrance, we are enabled to wait for God to act. However, we must also acknowledge that even though we process our pain through lament, healing and restoration may not happen in this lifetime. In fact, there are several psalms that don't conclude with praise or confidence.[24] This doesn't mean that we lose hope in our waiting. We can remain hopeful, even in the midst of suffering. As Henri Nouwen notes, "Hope is not dependent on peace in the land, justice in the world, and success in the business. Hope is willing to leave unanswered questions unanswered and unknown futures unknown. Hope makes you see God's guiding hand not only in the gentle and pleasant moments but also in the shadows of disappointment and darkness."[25]

Rather than displaying passive resignation or navel-gazing stagnation, when we lament we are exhibiting faith in God. This faith ultimately leads us to a hopeful willingness to surrender ourselves and our circumstances to him. In other words, the purpose of lament is so we can live with active expectation and trust in God, not cynicism. Pouring out our pain, doubt, anger, and disappointment leads to a renewed willingness to let God's will be done in our lives and the lives of those around us.

REFLECTION QUESTIONS

We have explored the purpose of lament according to the following three categories: to give voice to our pain, to provide an avenue to engage God, and ultimately to lead us into greater hope.

---

[23]Claus Westermann, *Praise and Lament in the Psalms* (Atlanta: John Knox, 1981), 257.
[24]Ps 38; 39; 44; 60; 80; 88; 89; 90.
[25]Henri Nouwen, *Turn My Mourning into Dancing: Finding Hope in Hard Times* (Nashville: Thomas Nelson, 2004), 54.

The Purpose of Lament

1. How have these categories helped to inform your view of lament?
2. Why is giving voice to our pain important? Do you practice lament in your own life? If not, reflect why you do not do so, for example, fear of judgment, emotions that are too overwhelming, and so on.
3. What communal lament practices have you observed in your church? How can church communities practice communal lament better? What are some practical steps we can take to stand alongside those who are suffering?
4. We generally let only those who are closest to us know our real thoughts. How can you be more honest in your prayers?
5. How does lament lead to hope? Why is it important to reflect on whom we are lamenting to? What character traits of God enable us to lament before him?

INDIVIDUAL PRACTICE

Take some time to practice lament. Make a conscious decision to not let distractions and busyness crowd out your time with God. Keep in mind the purposes of lament discussed in this chapter and invite God into spaces that you are struggling with or that are painful. These may even be things you have pushed away because they were too difficult to face. Spend some time remembering God and his character. If you have not prayed in a while, just mediate on God as your Heavenly Father—that he wants you to come to him with your burdens, doubts, and pain. Read Scripture, for example, parts of the book of Psalms, and then allow yourself to just sit in silence. Journal, pray, or draw the elements from the lament genre that you have learned. Try to personalize these elements if you can. Ask God to give you perspective on your pain. Remember that this is a process and not a one-time practice.

CORPORATE PRACTICE

What are some issues that your community is dealing with or has dealt with recently? Can you take some time in a service to lament corporately, or even have a separate service? Suggest this idea to the church and ask people to be prayer and even fast for the corporate time of lament. Give enough lead time so that hearts are prepared. Consider having some members who are willing to organize the time include songs of lament and/or write out a prayer of lament that could be read and prayed collectively. Personal testimonies can also be helpful. After the service, have small group leaders follow up with their members about this time.

PART 2

Practicing Lament for Various Situations

5

Lament and Sin/Repentance

This chapter begins the second half of the book, which will cover more practical application of lament for specific situations. Each chapter in this section will discuss how the practice of lament plays an important role in various situations and will also examine specific examples of the lament genre in Scripture. I will give attention to the different elements used as well as provide some practical applications. Examples both from the Bible and individuals' lives are not meant to be exhaustive. They are only given to provide guidance and illustrate how lament can be a useful tool for Christian life today.

This chapter will focus on sin and repentance. While not all prayers of lament discuss sin or repentance, there are some that deal with this topic in greater detail, for example Psalms 38; 51; 130. Some Old Testament scholars, such as Lena-Sofia Tiemeyer, argue that prayers of repentance are actually a separate genre/category of prayer called penitential prayers, while others, such as Mark Boda, see a development in later Hebrew prayers that displays a transition from communal laments to penitential prayers.[1] Still others, such as Bruce Waltke, view penitential prayers as a

---

[1]See Lena-Sofia Tiemeyer, "The Doubtful Gain of Penitence: The Fine Line Between Lament and Penitential Prayer," in *Spiritual Complaint: The Theology and Practice of Lament*, ed. Miriam J. Bier and Tim Bulkeley (Cambridge: Clarke, 2013), 102-22. There are seven psalms considered penitential: Ps 6; 32; 38; 51; 102; 130; 143; Mark J. Boda, "The Priceless Gain of Penitence: From Communal Lament to Penitential Prayer in the 'Exilic' Liturgy of Israel," *Horizons in Biblical Theology* 25 (2003): 51-75; Richard J. Bautch, *Developments in Genre Between Post-exilic Penitential Prayers and*

subcategory. He writes, "One subcategory of lament psalms is the penitential lament, psalms that make confession of and lament sin. The lament form remains, only the subject matter is not personal adversity but moral failure."[2]

SIN IN THE BIBLE

Broadly speaking, sin can be categorized into three main groupings: sins we commit against others, whether God or fellow human beings; sins committed against us; and sin that is a result of fallen human nature and creation. This chapter will primarily deal with lament and repentance as pertains to sins we commit against God or fellow human beings. Patrick Miller describes well this type of sin: "Sin is not finally, and in the Bible never actually, an abstract notion. It is a warp in the divine order, a breakdown in the nature of relationship, a moral breach that always has consequences, however small they may be, and damages the way things are meant to be among ourselves and with God."[3]

Have you ever acted in a way that you knew was clearly going against what God wanted you to do, for example, lying, cheating, slandering, boasting, hurting others, refusing to forgive, or clinging to something you knew God was calling you to surrender? These actions have a way of creating rifts in our relationship with God and our relationships with others. Sometimes they may even become the root of a cold and callous response to other things that God is speaking to us. If we find ourselves one day so far from God and others that we do not even understand how we got there, chances are we have given sin a stronghold. The Bible likens sin to leaven or yeast that can quickly spread through a whole batch of dough. New Testament passages such as Luke 12:1 warn against the leaven (sin) of hypocrisy. Similarly, Paul

---

the Psalms of Communal Lament (Leiden: Brill, 2003). The purpose of this chapter is not to distinguish between or discuss the development of laments and penitential prayers but rather to discuss how laments in general can be applied to situations where sin is present and is incorporated into the process of lament.

[2]Bruce K. Waltke and Fred G. Zaspel, *How to Read and Understand the Psalms* (Wheaton, IL: Crossway, 2023), 275.

[3]Patrick D. Miller, *They Cried to the Lord: The Form and Theology of Biblical Prayer* (Minneapolis: Fortress, 1994), 248.

warns the Corinthians against tolerating egregious sexual immortality in their fellowship because this influence could permeate the whole church (1 Cor 5:1-8).

When sin is present, relationships are strained and can even be broken, and therefore acknowledgment and confession of sin through lament is important in the process of restoration. While confession of sin in the Bible is not always linked to lament (e.g., Solomon's temple prayer; see 1 Kings 8:46-51), there are obvious links in the prophets, Lamentations, and Psalms as well as some New Testament passages. For example, the prophet Amos calls the people to lament and repent over their sins (Amos 5:17). Hosea 10:5 speaks of how the Northern Kingdom of Israel will lament over their idolatry because they will be exiled. The lament in Lamentations 1:18 speaks of the Lord's righteousness in the light of Jerusalem's rebellion, and the psalmist in Psalm 130 laments over his sin and waits for restoration. Channing Crisler notes a link between lament and sin in Romans 7:7-25.[4] Similarly, 2 Corinthians 7:10 speaks of godly sorrow bringing repentance that leads to salvation. As New Testament believers, we know that Christ paid the penalty for sin once and for all (Heb 7:27); nevertheless, on this side of heaven, we continue to struggle with sin and are therefore called to confess so that we may be healed (Jas 5:16). Moreover, 1 John 1:9 says, "If we confess our sins, he is faithful and just to forgive us our sins and to cleanse us from all unrighteousness" (ESV).

As we saw in chapter three, in ancient Near Eastern prayers the act of confession was often aimed at warding off the wrath of the gods so that new blessings and deliverance might come. The Bible also speaks of this connection between sin and the wrath of God. Often, where sin is present, the wrath of God is also felt, either through his absence or through specific acts of judgment, for example exile. However, unlike the ancient Near Eastern gods, who were thought to be capricious in their anger, Yahweh's wrath is righteous. His response to confession does not indicate that he needs to be appeased because he is

---

[4]Channing L. Crisler, "The 'I' Who Laments: Echoes of Old Testament Lament in Romans 7:7-25 and the Identity of the ἐγώ," *Catholic Biblical Quarterly* 82, no. 1 (January 2020): 73.

offended. Instead, it is to be understood in the light of God's anger because

> a moral reality exists, and that reality seeks moral perfection, not simply a kind of satisfaction unrelated to what we know as a good and right and just. . . . Setting things right in the created and moral world God made happens in penitence as much as in judgment. It is not divine appetite that confessions seek to satisfy, but a divine nature that is just and insists that the universe reflects that justice.[5]

In other words, God's wrath is just because it stems from righteous anger when sin is involved. Confession and lament are seeking to bring shalom back into God's created and moral world. Seen in this way, confession is not just acknowledgment of sin; it is also seeking forgiveness and mercy because it realizes the justice of God's wrath. Lament over sin is opening conversation with God to remember his covenant and restore the relationship. It is not first and foremost about avoiding punishment but rather about seeking reconciliation.

Among the individual laments, Psalm 51 is often quoted in reference to its dealing with sin and is instructive for situations where sin has been committed and reconciliation is sought.[6] This psalm is most commonly associated with King David. More specifically, this psalm is connected to the narrative of the prophet Nathan's confrontation of David concerning his adultery with Bathsheba and his subsequent cover-up plan involving the murder of her husband, Uriah (2 Sam 11–12). However, the psalm itself does not discuss these acts of sin with specificity. Most scholars believe that the historical note or superscription connecting it to David was added later.[7] Nevertheless, this psalm is applicable to David's situation and is also general enough to be applied to a variety of situations that pertain to sin or specific acts of sin that have been committed. Let us take a closer look at this psalm to see how it can be instructive for us.

---

[5]Miller, *They Cried to the Lord*, 248.
[6]Waltke and Zaspel, *How to Read*, 275-88. Like Waltke, I view penitential psalms like this one as a subcategory under the individual lament genre.
[7]For a discussion of psalm titles, see Peter C. Craigie and Barker, *Psalms 1–50*, 2nd ed., Word Biblical Commentary (Grand Rapids, MI: Zondervan Academic, 2016), 33-55.

Lament and Sin/Repentance

PSALM 51

For the director of music. A psalm of David. When the prophet Nathan came to him after David had committed adultery with Bathsheba.

Have mercy on me, O God,
    according to your unfailing love;
according to your great compassion
    blot out my transgressions.
Wash away all my iniquity
    and cleanse me from my sin.
For I know my transgressions,
    and my sin is always before me.
Against you, you only, have I sinned
    and done what is evil in your sight;
so you are right in your verdict
    and justified when you judge.
Surely I was sinful at birth,
    sinful from the time my mother conceived me.
Yet you desired faithfulness even in the womb;
    you taught me wisdom in that secret place.
Cleanse me with hyssop, and I will be clean;
    wash me, and I will be whiter than snow.
Let me hear joy and gladness;
    let the bones you have crushed rejoice.
Hide your face from my sins
    and blot out all my iniquity.
Create in me a pure heart, O God,
    and renew a steadfast spirit within me.
Do not cast me from your presence
    or take your Holy Spirit from me.
Restore to me the joy of your salvation
    and grant me a willing spirit, to sustain me.
Then I will teach transgressors your ways,
    so that sinners will turn back to you.
Deliver me from the guilt of bloodshed, O God,
    you who are God my Savior,
    and my tongue will sing of your righteousness.

> Open my lips, Lord,
>   and my mouth will declare your praise.
> You do not delight in sacrifice, or I would bring it;
>   you do not take pleasure in burnt offerings.
> My sacrifice, O God, is a broken spirit;
>   a broken and contrite heart
>   you, God, will not despise.
> May it please you to prosper Zion,
>   to build up the walls of Jerusalem.
> Then you will delight in the sacrifices of the righteous,
>   in burnt offerings offered whole;
>   then bulls will be offered on your altar.

Recall that the following five elements are characteristic of laments. As mentioned before, not all elements will be present in every lament, and they may not follow this order.

- address or invocation
- lamentation/petition/complaint
- motivations
- confession of trust/assurance of being heard
- vow of praise

Address or invocation. Before addressing the various elements of lament in Psalm 51, it will be helpful to comment on its structure. This psalm has proved difficult to outline, and scholars offer various reasons for this. For example, Artur Weiser argues that a lack of "homogeneous construction" of this psalm is due to "the distress of the life of prayer out of which the psalm has arisen."[8] Other scholars, though they would agree that a simple structure is hard to discern, still observe some obvious ordering through the use of keywords and themes. Anthony Ceresko, for example, observes a chiastic arrangement of keywords in Psalm 51:3-11 focusing specifically on Psalm 51:6b, which declares God's blamelessness when he judges.[9]

---

[8] Artur Weiser, *The Psalms*, Old Testament Library (Louisville, KY: Westminster John Knox, 1962), 401.
[9] Anthony R. Ceresko, "The Function of Chiasmus in Hebrew Poetry," *Catholic Biblical Quarterly* 40, no. 1 (January 1978): 6.

Just as we can observe structural correspondences, we can also see the lament elements identified in chapter three as present in this psalm. The psalmist begins with a cry for mercy addressed to God. He also appeals to God's steadfast love and mercy. Engaging with God is the first step of any lament, and taking this step shows that we recognize that God is the one to whom we can turn for help and forgiveness. The psalm also shows a recognition and acknowledgment of who the God of the Bible is. Yahweh is not just any god; he is a God of steadfast love and abundant mercy. The terms for steadfast love (*ḥesed*) and mercy (*raḥămîm*) used here are the same terms used for God's characteristics when he reveals himself to Moses in Exodus 34 on Mount Sinai. In that passage, God allows Moses to get a glimpse of his glory and shows him that he is merciful (*raḥûm*, adjectival form) and abounding in steadfast love (see Ex 34:6). It is also because of his steadfast love that he keeps forgiving transgressions and sins, for even a thousand generations (see Ex 34:7).

Notice that the psalmist is not appealing to God's omnipotence or omnipresence, even though these are attributes we often associate with God. Instead, the psalmist shows that he is aware that forgiveness of sin is predicated on God's steadfast love and his mercy. Moreover, the first verb in Psalm 51:2 [3] is asking for favor.[10] The Hebrew term *honnēnî* here, "be merciful to me," expresses the desire for action from a superior to an inferior. More specifically, it is asking for unmerited or undeserved favor. This is important because when we approach God full of sin and shame, we must remember that God is not is a drill sergeant or a cosmic policeman out to get us for every violation we have committed. No, he is a God of steadfast love and mercy. He is the one to whom we can come for unmerited favor. Romans 2:4 also acknowledges that it is God's kindness that leads us to repentance.

Appealing for favor based on God's steadfast love and mercy not only highlights God's character but also emphasizes the covenant relationship with Yahweh. The term *ḥesed* ("steadfast love") is closely associated with God's covenant with his people. Noting these associations in the initial

---

[10]The brackets here and elsewhere indicate the verse number in the Hebrew Bible (Masoretic Text). In some places the Masoretic Text's versification differs from that in English translations.

verses is important because it reminds us that the psalmist is coming before God with confidence in an already-existent covenant relationship. As New Testament believers, we can also come before God for forgiveness with even greater assurance because of what Jesus has done on the cross. Hebrews 4:16 reminds us as people of the new covenant that we can come with confidence before God's "throne of grace, that we may receive mercy and find grace help in time of need." When we are lamenting sin in our lives, we do not come before God with uncertainty. No! Instead, because of Christ's death and resurrection, we can come with hope. This is an encouraging reminder because the condemnation of sin can sometimes feel louder than the confidence we have in the cross of Christ.

Lamentation/petition/complaint. This psalm does not contain a complaint, primarily because the psalmist is acknowledging sin and not blame shifting. Beginning with Psalm 51:2-3 [3-4], there is a series of four petitions or commands, asking God to "have mercy," "wipe away" transgression, "wash" iniquity, and "cleanse" sin. These commands or imperative verbs continue in Psalm 51:11-12 with another series of four command verbs that ask God to "hide" his face from the psalmist's sin, to "wipe away" his iniquity, and ultimately to "create" a clean heart and to "make anew" or "renew" the spirit within him. Notice that the progression of these verbs begins with God's mercy, then moves to petitions for cleansing or removal of the old, and culminates with a new creation or making anew. The Hebrew verb *māḥāh*, "to blot out," is used in Psalm 51:1 [3] and at the end of Psalm 51:9 [11], closing out the psalmist's request for cleansing. This verb most likely refers to the act of erasing from a scroll or tablet. In other words, the psalmist is asking for a clean slate. The two subsequent verbs in Psalm 51:2 refer more to the washing of clothes, as in Jeremiah 2:22, and physical cleaning or ritual cleansing (Lev 11:32). By using all three terms, the psalmist is asking for God to cleanse him thoroughly.

Marvin Tate notes, "The three verbs for forgiveness are matched by three prime words for sin פשע, עון, and חטא in vv 1-2 [3-4]."[11] While these

---

[11] Marvin E. Tate, *Psalms 51–100*, Word Biblical Commentary (Nashville: Thomas Nelson, 1991), 15.

different terms for sin have some particular distinctions, they often overlap in their definitions and are most likely used to present a comprehensive view of sin. The psalmist is asking for thorough cleansing from the comprehensive nature of sin. This desire is further emphasized through the psalmist's confession that he is fully aware of his sins (Ps 51:4 [5]). However, he does not stop at acknowledgment but also laments that at the core, his actions went against God and caused a breach in their relationship. He then affirms God's blamelessness in his judgment (Ps 51:5 [6]). This admittance goes beyond mere physical acts of sin that have been committed and acknowledges that the psalmist was born with a sinful nature. The psalmist recognizes that his sinful actions were not just a one-time occurrence that was atypical of his normal course of action. Instead, he sinned because he is a sinner with a sinful nature.

However, this confession does not end in hopelessness and dejection. The psalmist is not wallowing in his sin or even over his sinful nature. Instead, he recognizes that God can teach wisdom to one who exhibits truth (ʾĕmet) because God delights in truth. As one scholar writes, "The word *emet* or truth emphasizes reliability and trustworthiness over absolute accuracy. God is seeking a person whose external profession is consistent with the inner reality of his or her being that is often kept hidden away in the inner parts."[12] This is important because God is not seeking perfection but wholeness. He desires for his people to be in right relationship with him and with one another, which is central to Israel's covenant obligations.[13]

In confession of sin, we must come with vulnerability and humility, not only acknowledging the specific acts we have committed, but also recognizing our wayward hearts. We must be willing to be honest and transparent before God and even ourselves. It is hard to face the depravity in

---

[12]Gerald Henry Wilson, *Psalms: The NIV Application Commentary from Biblical Text to Contemporary Life*, The NIV Application Commentary (Grand Rapids, MI.: Zondervan, 2002), 687.

[13]The covenant relationship Israel has with God goes back to Abraham (Gen 12:1) and extends into the covenant obligations of the Mosaic covenant (Ex 19–24 as well as the book of Deuteronomy). At the center of Israel's covenant obligations is to love God and love one another. The nation continued to neglect its covenant obligations, resulting in God's judgment and exile. For a fuller discussion, see Peter J. Gentry and Stephen J. Wellum, *God's Kingdom Through God's Covenants: A Concise Biblical Theology* (Wheaton, IL: Crossway, 2015), 93-206.

our own hearts. We do not want to see the ugliness of our actions and attitudes toward God and others. However, it is only when we are willing to openly and honestly lament and confess our sins that we can truly find cleansing and even renewal or change of heart.

A few years ago, I watched an interview of Steven Goff, who surrendered to the police of Galloway Township, New Jersey, for the murder of his childhood friend, which he committed when he was eighteen. Goff stabbed Frederick Hart several times behind the Clubs Condominiums in Galloway Township in 1990. He was never caught and tried to move on and live a normal life. However, twenty-three years later, Goff walked into the Galloway Township police station to confess his crime. Before turning himself in, he confided to a friend that "he was going to meet his maker and fess up to what he had done."[14] When asked what made him come forward, he replied,

> I couldn't live with myself; to be honest with you. It was tearing me apart. . . . The guilt became overwhelming. I couldn't eat, I couldn't sleep. It consumed me. It was twenty-three years ago . . . but it just seems that as time went on it was overwhelming. It was to a point where I became dysfunctional. It was just unhealthy to keep dealing with it anymore. I just had enough. I just couldn't let it tear me apart. I had to answer for what I did and his family needs closure. They are entitled to it. . . . When you clear your conscience for something. It does something for your soul. I feel like I have grown emotionally in the last couple of days. I know that sounds crazy or preposterous, but even though I am a killer, I feel like a am a better man today than I have ever been in my life. And I mean that because I have faced my demons. You know, I had this beat. I did. There was nobody who was going to catch me for this. I could have gone on for the rest of my life with this. But you know what; every time I put a razor to my face and shave and look in the mirror. I know.[15]

---

[14]Jessica Jerreat, "'You Deserve to See Me Suffer: Guilt-Ridden Hedge Fund Manager Who Confessed to 1990 Murder of Teenage Boy Is Sentenced to 30 Years in Prison,'" *Daily Mail*, July 19, 2013, www.dailymail.co.uk/news/article-2370582/Steven-Goff-aspiring-hedge-fund-manager-confessed-1990-murder-teenage-boy-sentenced-30-years-prison.html.

[15]Lynda Cohen and Anjalee Khelmani, "Exclusive Interview: Guilt 'Overwhelming' Says Man Who Confessed to Cold-Case Galloway Murder," *The Press of Atlantic City*, April 4, 2013, https://pressofatlanticcity.com/news/article_d16937b8-9c95-11e2-b533-001a4bcf887a.html.

Confession brings wholeness. Even if we do not face external consequences for our sins, our conscience does not rest. We must be willing to honestly confess, even if that means facing the consequences before God and others.

Motivations. The psalmist appeals to two motivations for God's forgiveness. First is for God to act according to his lovingkindness (*ḥesed*) and his abundant mercy (*raḥămîm*; Ps 51:2 [3]). As mentioned above, he is appealing to God to act according to his character. The second motivation is given in Psalm 51:3 [4] through the usage of the Hebrew conjunction *kî*, which most translations render "for." Oftentimes when this word is translated as "for," it provides the reason or motivation for acting on the preceding expression or expressions. In other words, by using this word to introduce Psalm 51:3 [4], the psalmist is using his recognition of wrongdoing and sin as a reason for God to act in Psalm 51:4-6 [5-7]. As he humbles himself before God in confession, he is hoping this will also motivate God to action. This concept is in complete alignment with Solomon's prayer in 2 Chronicles 7:14, "If my people, who are called by my name, will humble themselves and pray and seek my face and turn from their wicked ways, then I will hear from heaven, and I will forgive their sin and will heal their land."

Additionally, this motivation is strengthened with the repetition of the same Hebrew word translated "for" in Psalm 51:16 [18]. This verse stresses that God does not delight in sacrifices or whole burnt offerings. Instead, what God truly desires is a broken and contrite heart, as affirmed in Psalm 51:17 [19]. God is not motivated or appeased by mere ritual sacrifices. We do not bargain with God to motivate him to forgive through sacrifices that we bring. As New Testament believers, we may not bring literal animal sacrifices before God, but we may still try to bargain through other means. We may be inclined to tell God that we will start doing something, for example, praying, reading the Bible, going to church, if he will do what we request. Doing these actions is not wrong, but when we try to use them as leverage for bargaining with God, we are merely offering them as sacrifices with a transactional mentality. Lament is not to be viewed as another ritual act. It is not a formula or something we need to perform.

Confession of trust/assurance of being heard. This part of a lament usually indicates a shift in the disposition of the lamenter. A confession of trust consists of the psalmist's expression of confidence in God. In this psalm, the expression of confidence is found in Psalm 51:17 [19], where the psalmist is affirming the motivation expressed earlier— namely, his recognition that God does not despise a broken spirit or contrite heart. These statements indicate the psalmist's confidence that his request will be heard. While this transition is subtle, it does show that through his prayer, contemplation of God's character, and his own contrition, the psalmist can be hopeful that he will not be rejected. Furthermore, this recognition is followed by requests to rebuild and restore Jerusalem so that right sacrifices from renewed citizens can be offered. Tate views these final two verses in the psalm as later additions.[16] However, whether they are later additions or not, these verses show a greater confidence not only concerning the psalmist's own situation, but also for God's greater work in and through his people.

How does this element of lament play out in our own lives? As mentioned earlier, the shift from lament to greater hope is not always quantifiable or easy to trace, even in the Psalms themselves. There is no single explanation for the change in mood, but in this psalm the psalmist seems to be recalling God's character and drawing from what he knows to be true about God. For instance, he knows that God does not only desire sacrifices or whole burnt offerings, or the psalmist would provide these things (Ps 51:16 [18]), but instead God desires humility. While we may not always experience a quick change in mood when we meditate on God's character, we can hold fast to the truth that, even in sin, when we humble ourselves, God will respond. James 4:6-10 expresses a similar truth for us as New Testament believers:

---

[16]Tate, *Psalms 51–100*, 29.

> But he gives more grace. Therefore, it says, "God opposes the proud but gives grace to the humble." Submit yourselves therefore to God. Resist the devil, and he will flee from you. Draw near to God, and he will draw near to you. Cleanse your hands, you sinners, and purify your hearts, you double-minded. Be wretched and mourn and weep. Let your laughter be turned to mourning and your joy to gloom. Humble yourselves before the Lord, and he will exalt you. (ESV)

In our humility and lament, God will bring a time of exaltation. We can bank on that. For those of us who are dealing with a guilty conscience or unconfessed sin, let us fill our minds with the truth of God's character and his promises. He will not reject us. Even though we may be burdened now, full of grief and remorse, God will forgive. Let us humble ourselves along with the psalmist and wait on the Lord for his renewed work in our hearts in the knowledge that he does not reject us when we come before him with all our brokenness.

Vow of praise. This component is listed last in the discussion of chapter three, but in this psalm it comes before the confession of trust/assurance of being heard. As stated earlier, this element is often closely associated with the assurance of being heard, confession of trust, or experienced deliverance. Here the psalmist offers a vow to praise in Psalm 51:14-15 [16-17] after his final plea for personal deliverance from his sin, more specifically his guilt of bloodshed. He vows to sing of Yahweh's righteousness and to declare his praise. Along with this, the psalmist declares that he will teach transgressors his ways so that others will also turn back. This vow indicates that the psalmist is not only concerned for his own sins to be forgiven. This is not the end goal. He desires for God to forgive and to bring restoration to him so that he can bring restoration to others. The overflow of a forgiven heart cannot be contained. This is a beautiful picture to keep in mind when we lament our sins. The ultimate purpose is not just to obtain forgiveness and restoration. It is to make us whole so that we can be part of God's bigger plan and purposes. Our hope is not just in restoration for ourselves but also for God's larger plan. The vow to praise and to turn others back is not to be seen here as a tactic to motivate God but rather the overflow of restoration and a renewed heart.

Jesus says in Luke 7:36-50 that the one who recognizes their sins and receives forgiveness will express greater love. The Pharisee did not express any gratitude because he did not see his own sins, while the "sinful" woman washed Jesus' feet with her tears. Jesus declares, "Therefore, I tell you, her many sins have been forgiven—as her great love has shown. But whoever has been forgiven little loves little. Then Jesus said to her, 'Your sins are forgiven'" (Lk 7:47-48). The point is not that the Pharisee is any more righteous than the woman and therefore needs only a little forgiveness. Instead, Jesus is showing that when we truly see our sins and recognize what he has done, we will not be able to restrain our response of worship. Like the psalmist, our vow of praise should be an expected overflow of the forgiveness we have already received in Christ.

Have you ever met a new Christian who is so grateful to be delivered from their previous life of sin that they cannot help but tell everyone around about what Christ has done? The response is not a drudgery or calculated, but an overflow that is contagious. I recently heard about a man who shared how Jesus saved him from a life of addiction, selling drugs, prostitution, and depression. He is now full of joy and wants others to know the freedom and healing they can receive in Christ. He expressed how he is grateful every day to share Christ and to do it for God's glory. We see this type of response time and time again in the Gospels. In the same way, when we lament and seek restoration, we must not just stop when we feel that reassurance of forgiveness. We must let it overflow so that we can help others know that they too can experience freedom and the love of God through forgiveness. Nathan's story below shows the power of lament and forgiveness.

Nathan's Story

My name is Nathan, and I am a twenty-four-year-old student at Taylor University. The pathway that brought me to Taylor was radically different from most students who attend because my personal story is filled with suffering and lament.

At the ripe age of twenty-one, I was freshly out of a wrongful relationship that I had been in for seven years. I was addicted to marijuana, I was an alcoholic, and I was doing various other street drugs. Additionally, I was hooked on the party scene. I would go out on the town at least three times a week, slowly wearing down my mind and body. Despite all this insanity and poor decision-making, I was able to hold down a full-time job as a concrete worker. I was a young man living however I deemed fit, but I was a shadow of the potential that I already knew God had placed within me. I had grown up in a strong Christian home, but this same home also had major traumatic events such as divorce and dissension.

At this time, I was angry with God over the death of eight of my friends in the span of three years. Four of these friends died of drug overdose, and the other four died from drug- or gang-related gun violence. These major events had caused me to misdirect the anger I held toward God, causing me to ask questions of basic theodicy. This sets the context for my story of lament and suffering with God.

On December 10, 2021, I was working on a job site on a large building extension. I oversaw the crew at this job site, and I released everyone to go to lunch. I decided to go to McDonald's and get a McChicken. As I was driving back to work, I accidentally crashed my car into a tree head-on. When I hit the tree, I had no seat belt on, and I was going about fifty miles an hour. Long story short, I ended up breaking my pelvis into twelve pieces. I broke my right arm almost in half, and I broke all the ribs on the right side of my body. I also broke my ankle and had a deep laceration on my knee. After three surgeries and about two months in the hospital, I was radically different. When I was in the hospital, I had to learn to walk all over again at the age of twenty-two and sustained major nerve damage that will most likely bring me great challenges for my entire life. All these crippling things that happened to me reduced me to the lowest point I have ever been in my life.

One important thing to note about the way I thought about God at this age was that I never doubted his existence because of prior experiences I had experienced as a young man. While in the hospital I questioned God relentlessly. I would ask things in prayer such as, "How could you have ever let something like this happen to me?" or, "If you are so good, how could you let me be a cripple for my whole life?" Despite the way these questions sound, there was a humbleness in the tone and heart in all of them. Looking back, I feel that my absolute level of brokenness assisted in the humble nature of these questions. After some time in the hospital, it came time for me to leave, but there was a major issue. My dad worked very long and demanding hours, and at the time my mother worked nights. These two factors led to my not having a place to stay that would provide adequate care for my health issues.

With not many options on the table, God intervened. The mother of one of my friends who had passed away when I was nineteen decided to visit me in the hospital and offered to take me in and take care of me for as long as I needed. I cannot express how grateful I am for her selfless care for me during this time. Because I was unable to get up and walk around by myself, she would help me get up and move me anytime I needed. She would take me almost daily to doctor and physical therapy appointments. She would assist me in eating, getting cleaned up, and anything else I desired. Keep in mind that the only tie this woman had to me was that I and her son were best friends before his death. While I was staying with her, we had various conversations about the death of her son, how it affected her, and her relationship with God. We also spoke about my feelings of anger and frustration toward God because of what had happened to me and the friends I had lost, including her own son.

When we were speaking there was a healing taking place in my own heart. God had somehow sent this grieving mother to take care of me in the most radical ways both physically and spiritually. She shared the pain she felt because of her son's death. When she shared this pain with me, she also shared that she never ever left God through all the suffering. The quality and love that was displayed to me in her character despite suffering an even deeper loss than I had humbled me to the core of my being. During the greatest suffering in my life, God sent an individual who had suffered well to teach me the same principles. Through her God showed me the glory that is revealed when we decide to lean on God wholeheartedly during senseless suffering and loss.

After leaving her home, I returned to stay with my dad in Farmland, Indiana. My dad has a rule in his household that if you live under his roof, you go to church on Sunday. Wanting to honor my dad, I began attending church again for the first time in three years. I would attend on Sunday mornings and also Wednesday night prayer services. On a random, not-so-spectacular Wednesday night prayer service, an older gentleman from the congregation was praying, and the power of God hit me like a missile going Mach 10. I began to cry, and I felt the weight of all my sins in one moment. I felt the shame of all the reckless and selfish decisions I had made in my life. Just as fast as all this shame and pain came into my heart, I felt a peace calm the storm that was raging within me. In that moment I knew God was calling me back into his arms. I knew at that moment that the only way to be rid of this pain and regret was through repenting to God. In that moment I publicly confessed, asked God to help me to never revert to my old ways, and committed myself to going after God's will for my life. As a result, I began working in the church again in worship ministry, camp ministry, youth ministry, and a handful of speaking opportunities. God immediately began to use the long lament process I had just undergone by using my testimony to show his glory.

After a couple of months, God made it very apparent to me through a variety of methods that I was to pursue vocational ministry and ministry education. This revelation and confirmation led me to enroll in Taylor University, at the age of twenty-three, after dropping out of school almost three years earlier. I am now pursuing my bachelor's in Christian ministry and am looking forward to growing in loving God and people better every day. Through lament and the help of a servant of God, God redeemed my life.

REFLECTION QUESTIONS

1. Is there sin in your life that is hindering your relationship with God or others?
2. How is lament in Psalm 51 instructive for you? What element of lament in this psalm is particularly helpful?
3. When we lament, the end goal is not just to obtain forgiveness and restoration. It is to make us whole so that we can be part of God's

bigger plan and purposes. How does this framework affect your perspective on repentance and forgiveness?

INDIVIDUAL PRACTICE

Read slowly over Psalm 51. What element in this lament stands out to you at this moment? Take some time to repent before the Lord of any sin or things that may be hindering your relationship with him or others. As you seek God's forgiveness, make sure to deal with any unforgiveness that you may have toward others as well. Sit in silence and ask the Lord whether there are any steps of restitution that you need to make. Write out the verses in Psalm 51 that stood out to you and put them on a notecard or take a picture on your phone. Review these verses throughout the day and pray them in your heart.

CORPORATE PRACTICE

Set aside some time during a worship service for the confession of sin for the purpose of reconciliation with God and others. Read Psalm 51 aloud and offer an opportunity for people to pray in silence alone or with another individual if reconciliation is necessary. Close this time with a song of confession and worship.

6

Lament and Doubt/Questions

I read an article published a few years ago titled, "Why Doubt Is Essential to Science in Scientific America."[1] The author concludes that sometimes doubts lead to greater discoveries. She argues that doubts are not weaknesses; instead, they can lead to new knowledge, better understanding, and new questions. This is also true of our faith. Too often we have come to believe that our questions and doubts are wrong, that they can stunt our growth or even cause us to lose our faith. Instead, we ought to accept things as they have been taught to us because that is how we will remain true to our faith. But this is not what we find in Scripture. The prophets, psalmists, and other godly figures in the Bible raise honest questions and doubts.

For example, Moses expresses his doubts in Exodus 5:22-23 when Pharaoh responds negatively to his request to let Israel go. Moses is only obeying God, but Pharoah and the Israelites blame him for making things worse. Job expresses his questions and doubts throughout the book of Job (Job 3:11; 12:24). He does not understand why he is plagued with so much loss and illness when he has a clear conscience. The prophet Jeremiah also complains to God about his doubts because of his constant persecution amid his clear call to be

---

[1] Liv Grjebine, "Why Doubt Is Essential to Science," *Scientific American*, October 9, 2020, www.scientificamerican.com/article/why-doubt-is-essential-to-science/.

God's spokesman (Jer 20:7-8). Likewise, the prophet Habakkuk vents his doubts through questions about God's use of the Babylonians to punish his own people (Hab 1). In the New Testament, John the Baptist (Jn 11:15) doubts Jesus, and Thomas, one of Jesus' twelve disciples, doubts his resurrection (Jn 20:24-28), as do the two disciples on the road to Emmaus (Lk 24:13-35).

What is important to note is that amid their doubts, all these people bring their questions and complaints in prayer before God or speak them directly to Jesus.[2] They are not rebuked or chastised for bringing these questions, complaints, and doubts. Instead, through these interactions, they come to know God and Jesus in a different way. Even though their original expectations are shattered, they all gain insight that deepens their understanding of God and his ways.

Psalms also displays questions, complaints, and doubts (Ps 13:1; 22:1; 77:11-15). While these sorts of expressions abound in prayers of lament, Psalm 13 is particularly instructive as we examine lament in the midst of questions, complaints, and doubts.

PSALM 13

> How long, LORD? Will you forget me forever?
>   How long will you hide your face from me?
> How long must I wrestle with my thoughts
>   and day after day have sorrow in my heart?
>   How long will my enemy triumph over me?
> Look on me and answer, LORD my God.
>   Give light to my eyes, or I will sleep in death,
> and my enemy will say, "I have overcome him,"
>   and my foes will rejoice when I fall.
> But I trust in your unfailing love;
>   my heart rejoices in your salvation.
> I will sing the LORD's praise,
>   for he has been good to me.

---

[2]These biblical examples do not technically fall under the genre of lament, but they exhibit the element of lamentation/petition and complaint found in lament.

Lament and Doubt/Questions

Recall that the following five elements are characteristic of laments. As mentioned before, not all elements are present in every lament, and they may not follow in this order.

- address or invocation
- lamentation/petition/complaint
- motivations
- confession of trust/assurance of being heard
- vow of praise

Address or invocation. The psalm begins with a series of lamenting questions directed to Yahweh, which continues into the next verse. It is clear from the beginning that the psalmist is directing his prayer to the one he believes can answer him. What stands out in this address is the way the psalmist approaches God. He opens with a series of questions that display his struggle, doubt, and complaint about God's inaction and silence. He is not talking to others about God; instead, he is going directly *to* God and expressing his feelings. Even though the psalmist feels like God has hidden his face, he will still engage God in faith. He does not turn away from God because he senses God's absence, but rather presses into seeking God more directly. This is important for us to remember when we are facing doubts or questions in our own lives. Instead of suppressing our doubts or questions, we need to press in and come before God in prayer. We must embrace the freedom to express these thoughts and feelings in our prayers.

Lamentation/petition/complaint. Here we see the psalmist's complaint expressed through questions about God's absence, as well as the psalmist's struggle with sorrow that is most likely brought about through his enemies. These cries are honest and direct. The interrogative phrase "How long?" is repeated four times in these first two verses (Ps 13:2-3). The Hebrew phrase ʿad-ʾānâ, translated "How long?" occurs only twelve times in Scripture and is usually expressing complaints when used in the Psalms.[3] It is not a coincidence that Psalm 13 uses this phrase four times early on. While on

---

[3]Robert D. Haak, *Habakkuk* (Leiden: Brill, 1992), 30; Avraham Evan-Shoshan, *A New Concordance of the Bible* (Jerusalem: Kiryat Sefer, 1977), 831. The twelve occurrences are found in Ex 16:28; Num 14:11; Josh 18:3; Jer 47:6; Hab 1:2; Ps 13:2 (2×); 13:3 (2×); 64:2; Job 18:2; 19:2.

the surface this interrogative phrase appears to be seeking information, Francis Andersen notes that questions of this type are "requests for information only in postexilic works (e.g., Ezra and Nehemiah); elsewhere they are always rhetorical and, moreover, accusatory."[4]

It is significant that the opening questions of Psalm 13 are rhetorical in nature. Research on rhetorical questions shows that when they are used, they can serve several different functions, even simultaneously.[5] First, they can be used by a speaker to highlight the obvious response. In other words, this type of question requires no answer since the speaker and/or the listener already knows the answer. Second, they can be used to make an emphatic declaration or statement. In some cases, they are used to remind the hearer of some important information. Third, these types of questions can be used to courteously correct or chastise the listener. Fourth, these questions can function as a persuasive device. They persuade the person listening to frame the expected answer in their mind so that they agree with the speaker. For example, a lawyer could ask a jury, "Don't you think it is wrong to murder?" The lawyer is not asking for a real answer. It is safe to assume that everyone knows this is true. Instead, the lawyer is making a case for their client and trying to persuade the jury to side with the plaintiff. Finally, rhetorical questions can also be used to express emotions such as doubt, displeasure, exasperation, or reproach.

As I mentioned earlier, the functions of these questions are not always clearly delineated because they can also fall into multiple categories. For example, a rhetorical question can make a statement while simultaneously urging the addressee to action. Rhetorical questions can also function as both a question and as a statement. This is significant because, even though they are questions, they can express doubt, displeasure, or complaint. More importantly, rhetorical questions also indicate a desire for engagement. Here the psalmist is not complaining in a vacuum but rather seeking to engage Yahweh with his concerns. This desire to reach

---

[4] Francis I. Andersen, *Habakkuk*, Anchor Bible (New Haven, CT: Yale University Press, 2001), 108.
[5] May Young, "Asking God Tough Questions: The Use of Interrogatives in Habakkuk's First Chapter," in *Christianity and COVID-19*, ed. Chammah J. Kaunda, Atola Longkumer, Kenneth R. Ross, and Esther Mombo (London: Routledge, 2021), 79-88.

out to God, even when he seems deliberately silent, exemplifies the poet's faith. He is not willing to throw his hands up in despair and disengage but instead chooses to initiate interaction with God. Instead of walking away from God, he turns to him. This allows for honest struggle because the psalmist can wrestle with his doubts and the incongruity of what he experiences and what he thinks to be true theologically.

Similarly, rhetorical questions provide an avenue for protest while simultaneously leaving room for, as well as expressing, desire to see the current situation rectified. The honest, questioning faith of the psalmist does not lead to despair but to greater communion and commitment. This is why the psalm ends with a confession of trust and a vow of praise. These questions indicate that he wants to engage God in genuine covenant interaction. Viewed in this way, the series of four "How long?" questions at the beginning of Psalm 13 are not necessarily seeking information from Yahweh about how much longer the psalmist must wait. Instead, they are expressing a complaint. More specifically, the psalmist is expressing his exasperation for all the prayers that he has prayed. He is saying that it is altogether too long for God not to act and to leave him to handle this sorrow in his heart by himself as his enemy continues to triumph. The psalmist is complaining that God is not answering him. His complaint is probably not too far off from our own complaints when we feel that God is silent, not acting or changing our circumstances. When we feel this, we are probably also doubting that he is even listening or answering. This can be discouraging and cause frustration in our hearts.

The psalmist probably feels these same emotions and is therefore raising concerns about God's passivity. These are reproachful questions.[6] They function argumentatively to politely chastise God while simultaneously persuading him to action. This is especially emphasized in the final question

---

[6]This is also what Andrew Davies's study on the why questions in complaint psalms found. "Real, direct questioning of God's action occurs much less frequently. In fact, only one of a handful of clear-cut and unambiguous examples of specific questions clearly addressed Yahweh about a particular action." Davies, "My God . . . Why? Questioning the Action and Inaction of YHWH in the Psalms," in *Why? . . . How Long? Studies on Voice(s) of Lamentation Rooted in Biblical Hebrew Poetry*, ed. LeAnn Snow Flesher, Carol J. Dempsey, and Mark J. Boda (London: T&T Clark, 2013), 63. See Ps 80:12.

in Psalm 13:2 [3], which speaks of the triumph of the psalmist's enemy. By raising this rhetorical question, the psalmist is complaining about God's inaction toward injustice.

In the Psalms, when enemies are mentioned, they can refer to a variety of things, for example, false witnesses, other nations, ungodly people, and even illness or death. However, as the *Theological Dictionary of the Old Testament* notes, "The important thing is not the precise description of the enemies, but the theological classification of their work as contrary to God and chaotic."[7] In other words, the psalmist is simultaneously chastising God's tolerance and inactivity regarding the enemy who has risen up while also calling God to action. Even though the enemy is not clearly identified in this rhetorical question, the psalmist is insinuating that the enemy has the upper hand because of Yahweh's inaction. This is precisely why he is protesting and calling Yahweh to action.

Moreover, the psalmist's use of these rhetorical questions prevents him from making outright statements of accusation, indicating that he recognizes he is speaking with Yahweh, the Almighty God. In other words, by using rhetorical questions, the psalmist is simultaneously exhibiting faith and showing respect while honestly questioning. He knows that Yahweh is God and he is not, but at the same time he will not remain silent. The usage of the interrogative form or syntax of a question seems to be a deterrent from making outright accusations that would set the psalmist in the judgment seat above the God.

Last, these queries then lead into a petition in Psalm 13:3 [4] asking God to take notice and bring deliverance from the psalmist's sickness and grief. Here the enemy is partially identified. The phrase "the eyes were enlightened" signifies health (e.g., Deut 34:7); therefore, the psalmist is pleading for God to heal him. There is boldness in this lament. He is not giving up hope even though he feels God is distant. We can sense the psalmist's desperation to engage God in the midst of his pain and suffering.

---

[7]Helmer Ringgren, "אָיַב," in *Theological Dictionary of the Old Testament*, ed. G. Johannes Botterweck and Helmer Ringgren, trans. John T. Willis et al., vol. 1 (Grand Rapids, MI: Eerdmans, 1974–2006).

If you are facing times of discouragement because you do not see God moving or you are experiencing his silence, remember that, like the psalmist, you can also ask God questions. We do not have to sit in our discouragement and doubts; we can seek to engage God even when he seems silent. Remember, silence does not equate to absence. God is still there. Our prayers are not in vain, because God has given us an avenue to enter into his throne room (Heb 4:16). At the same time, we do not have to be disrespectful. Like the psalmist, we can remind God of his promises and plead with him to act accordingly.

Motivations. The psalmist appeals to God's compassion and justice. The enemy in Psalm 13:4 [5] is most likely referring to death, which is mentioned earlier in Psalm 13:3 [4]. This means the psalmist is asking God to save him lest death have the final word. Additionally, "the foes," in plural form in Psalm 13:4 [5], are most likely referring to the psalmist's physical enemies, who will taunt him if God does not deliver. Here the psalmist tries to motivate God to act so that the enemy and foes will not triumph. He is also appealing to his own helplessness and to God's mercy. Notice how these motivations are tied to what the psalmist knows to be true about God's character. Remember, we do not just come before God in honesty; we are also appealing to who he is. He is a God of compassion, justice, and mercy. Like the psalmist, in our doubts and complaints, we must also remind ourselves of the kind of God we are approaching. Who is it we are engaging in prayer? He is not callous and unconcerned. He is a God who cares (1 Pet 5:7). He is a God who understands our struggles (Heb 4:15). He is a God who knows our weaknesses (Ps 103:14). He is a God who knows the very number of hairs on our heads (Lk 12:7). He is not ignorant of our circumstances (Ps 33:18). As we approach God with our questions, doubts, and complaints, we must also remember who he is and that he loves us.

Confession of trust/assurance of being heard. The shift from Psalm 13:4 [5] to Psalm 13:5 [6] displays an obvious transition from lament to hope. While the text does not give specific reasons for this move, we can see it indicated through the word *but* combined with the first-person subject *I* at the beginning of Psalm 13:5 [6]. When the text displays this type of syntax, it indicates a move from lament to a confession of trust or assurance of being heard. In this psalm, the psalmist is making a confession of trust. He states, "But I trust in your unfailing love" (Ps 13:5 [6]). Again, God's unfailing love or ḥesed, which is associated with his character as mentioned in Exodus 34:6, is highlighted. The psalmist is stating that he has confidence because of who God is, namely, a God of unfailing love or ḥesed. The salvation the psalmist hopes for is based on the very character of God. The psalmist's hope and confidence are rooted in these statements about God in Psalm 13:5 [6].

When we doubt, question, or complain, there needs to come a time for us to reflect on God's character. Are we going to believe what God has revealed to us about himself in his Word, or are we going to let our doubts get the best of us? Remember that the serpent planted seeds of doubt in Eve so that she began to doubt God's good intentions (Gen 3:1). She started to believe the serpent that God was holding back and depriving her of the knowledge that the tree could give her. She forgot who God was, the one who created her and gave her such abundance. She downplayed the fact that she could eat of every tree except one and chose to focus on the tree that she could not have instead of focusing on the bounty God offered. Sometimes in our doubts, complaints and questions, we need to reorient our perspective. Is God really withholding? Is he really against us when he gave up his son for us (Rom 8:32)? Is he really a God who has abandoned us when he says he will never leave us or forsake us (Heb 13:5)? Like the psalmist, we must remember God's ḥesed, his unfailing love, and know that God saves and cares. We are not alone. God is not against us (Rom 8:31). God is just (Deut 32:25), and he is bigger than what we can imagine (Is 40:12-31).

We can think about our relationship with God like a relationship with a close friend or family member. If you have doubts about a friend or family member's concern and love for you, you can and should approach them in honesty, expressing your hurt, complaints, and questions. Instead of walking away or dismissing them as you would as a stranger or an acquaintance, you press in more because you have a long history and have built a foundation of love and trust. You may doubt their love

Lament and Doubt/Questions

because of actions or words they have spoken, but you know their character. How much more should this be true of God? We are not approaching a God who is merely an acquaintance or one who is distant and unaware of our situations. If we truly believe that the Bible is God's Word, we know that God is intimately aware of our situation and always intends the best for our lives.

Believing what the Bible says about God is a choice. Like the psalmist, who makes a deliberate choice to say "But I trust," this is something we must decide to do as well. After pouring out our hearts, we must decide to take God at his word or continue in our unbelief. This does not mean that our circumstances have changed or that we will not struggle, but it means that we are not going to let doubts, complaints, and questions have the final word. We must examine them in the light of God's character. We must compare them to what the Bible says about who God is. We must then choose faith and hope in light of these truths. Habakkuk is a great example of making this choice. The prophet begins the book asking God some tough rhetorical questions, but he ends the book with a psalm of trust and praise. More specifically, he says he will wait and even rejoice when he does not see any signs of change (Hab 3:16-18).

Vow of praise. The psalmist ends with a vow of praise to the Lord for his goodness in Psalm 13:6. What began with lamentation and complaint has progressed to a vow of praise. Just like Habakkuk, the psalmist ends with confidence. What is interesting is that his vow of praise is predicated on God's past goodness. "I will sing the Lord's praise, for he has been good to me." He remembers God's past goodness and uses it as a reason to trust. Like the psalmist, we do not have to remain in doubt. We can choose to remember God's past goodness to us. Even if our lives seem like they have no signs of goodness, we must come back to the foundational work of salvation. We must not define goodness merely as physical blessings or circumstances. God's goodness is so much deeper. It is the deliverance from sin and death that Jesus died to give us. God knew that this was our deepest need and that this was the best that he could give (Rom 8:32). Money, health, and a comfortable life pale in comparison. There are plenty of people who struggle even though they have these things. Optimal circumstances in this life are only temporary. Jesus died to give us eternal life with him. Alex's story will show that we can lament while ultimately trusting in God even when our circumstances are not comfortable.

Alex's Story

Whenever there is a lamenter, there is also a comforter. The very process of lament is not really complete without someone witnessing the lamentation. In my life, there was a period of great uncertainty regarding a matter of life and death. I was seeking political asylum from a dictatorial government. Statistically speaking, over 95 percent of asylum seekers get rejected for one reason or another, and applicants often hire very experienced lawyers to file their case and to represent them before Homeland Security. In my case, I had neither because I could not afford it. However, there was one Friend who stuck closer than a brother.

Naturally, I asked the Lord to help me stay in the United States. However, the prayer process was not without challenges. The biggest hurdle I had to face was all the religious views that certain Christians had given me about God. To be frank, some Christians seem to view God only as mean and dictatorial. What I mean by that is that people think God has sufferings planned for us, and we are to gladly receive them and try to come out of them with improved piety. Many only interpreted bad circumstances as "God teaching them a lesson," and so on. This perspective is seen as "spiritually mature" and often gets touted as the correct way to live in our relationship with God. While there are definitely times that God will discipline us out of love, he is also our deliverer and refuge. What I have realized in my time of trial is that unless we come to a scenario where it is about life and death, we will miss God as who he really is, a good Father.

When I was waiting for the asylum interview, I was not able to legally work. Can you imagine the mental stress for a person who has no means of livelihood while waiting on an uncertain decision that would forever change his life, for life or for death? Many Christians who do not know the good Father asked me questions such as, "What if God doesn't help you?" or "What if it's not God's will for you to stay here?" These questions created further conflict in my heart when it was hard to believe for such a miracle to begin with. The only thing that I relied on to not commit some sort of ultimate hopeless action was the small whisper in my heart about who the Lord really is. I was reminded about how he stopped at the funeral proceeding of the son of the widow from Nain; how he healed the ten lepers, knowing only one of them would come back and thank him; and how he was not willing to let the five thousand go without feeding them first. When I saw the Lord in those incidents, it made me realize what kind of person he is.

Of course, I lamented about my circumstance and how difficult it was to be without livelihood and without certainty about the future of my life. But my lamentation mattered because of the one who sees me. I had days when I thought of committing suicide because of the fear of not staying in this land. He did not rebuke my lack of faith but rather gently reminded me of his goodness, that he was determined to deliver me out of "Egypt" and bring me into my promised land. When I watched my savings dwindle and wondered how I was going to eat, he used lyrics from a hymn to assure me. "Before the throne of God of above I have a strong and perfect plea, a great High Priest whose name is Love, whoever lives and pleads for me. My name is graven on His hands; my name is written on his heart; I know that while in heav'n He stands, no tongue can bid me thence depart."[8]

Most asylum applicants wait for a long time. In fact, many have waited more than ten or fifteen years without getting an interview. I waited only six months before my interview was scheduled. And praise the Lord, I was granted asylum two days after the interview. I remember opening my mailbox and finding that orange-colored package. When I opened it on my table and found my asylum approval letter, I cried and realized that my ultimate purpose as a Christian is to know God's love like a friend knows a secret, like a child knows the Father. As I lamented through my questions and doubts, I was able to come honestly before my Heavenly Father and lean into the truth that he is loving and faithful.

---

[8] Charitie Lees Bancroft, "Before the Throne of God Above" (1863).

REFLECTION QUESTIONS

1. What are some doubts you have about God and his actions and inactions in your life?
2. How is the lament in Psalm 13 instructive for you? What element of lament is particularly helpful?
3. Why is it important to remember God's character and his actions in the past when we are facing doubts?
4. What steps do you need to take to trust God's word over your doubts?

INDIVIDUAL PRACTICE

Spend some time alone with God and write down some of the doubts you have about God or your situation as well as questions you have for him. Read over the following passages of Scripture that speak of God's goodness, power, character, and faithfulness in Christ's work for us: Isaiah 40; Job 41–42:6; Exodus 34:6-7; Romans 8:32-39; Hebrews 10:19-23. Voice your questions and doubts to God in prayer as you continue to hold these truths about God in your mind. If appropriate, dialogue with him about what you are experiencing and how it does not align with what you read. Allow space for yourself to wait on God and his timing. Allow the Holy Spirit to give you a renewed perspective on your circumstance. Journal or pray as you feel led. Even if you are not used to journaling, you may want to consider doing it because it allows us to trace the trajectory of our journeys with God.

CORPORATE PRACTICE

Provide a safe space for those who are doubting to share their doubts. This may be creating a small group designated for this purpose or scheduling time for these individuals to meet with a leader in the church over coffee. Give individuals time and space to share their burdens. Do not feel like you have to have answers at this time. Acknowledge their struggle and pray with them. If appropriate, read Psalm 22:1-5. Remind them that Jesus also prayed the first verse of this psalm in his darkest hour.

7

Lament and Injustice/Unfair Circumstances and Anger

When we think of lament, we often think of grief, sadness, and hopelessness. But an important part of lament in Scripture is anger. Often lament is an outworking of injustice and unfair circumstances in the world. Our world is filled with injustice and in many ways is not much different from the world of the psalmists. Whether violence, natural disasters, or war, injustice is present at every turn, often leaving us bewildered at why God seems to not be acting. If you are like me, you feel more than just overwhelmed. Perhaps you are angry that there are people who are willing to commit atrocities. Without an anchor in something outside ourselves, anger can very quickly turn to apathy or bitterness due to our feelings of helplessness amid evil. The lament psalms provide us a way to engage our anger at injustice in a constructive and ultimately hopeful way.

HOW TO THINK ABOUT IMPRECATORY PSALMS

Handling anger and injustice requires us to examine a subcategory of laments in the Psalms called imprecatory psalms. This type of psalm was crafted as a way to call a curse onto an enemy. I do not intend here to provide an exhaustive treatment of these psalms but enough of a context to help us understand how and why we can pray these psalms today.¹ Imprecatory psalms are laments that contain some harsh sentiments against enemies. For example, the psalmist cries out in Psalm 137:8-9:

> Daughter Babylon, doomed to destruction,
>   happy is the one who repays you
>   according to what you have done to us.
> Happy is the one who seizes your infants
>   and dashes them against the rocks.

The word *imprecation* comes from the Latin verb *imprecor*, which means "to invoke, call down, pray, utter curses." This subcategory of lament psalms is sometimes treated on its own as featuring its own shared elements.² Determining the actual number of psalms that fit into the imprecatory psalm genre is not straightforward. Most scholars would recognize the following as fitting this genre: Psalms 12; 58; 83; 129; 137, which are communal, and Psalms 69; 94; 109, which are individual.³ However, Psalm 94, which we will examine in this chapter, does not neatly fall into the category of an individual lament because the concerns addressed relate also to the community as a whole, even though first-person *I* and *me* forms are used later in the poem. Additionally, the poem ends with the first-person plural form *our*, referring to the community.

Clearly the number of imprecatory laments that fall into the communal or corporate category is greater than those that are individual in nature. This is instructive because we must remember that this type of language is not something we invoke lightly. We should not be praying imprecatory words against the person who took our parking space or who cut in front of us at the coffee shop. These psalms are usually dealing with situations

---

¹See Trevor Laurence, *Cursing with God: The Imprecatory Psalms and the Ethics of Christian Prayer* (Waco, TX: Baylor University Press, 2022); David G. Firth, *Surrendering Retribution in the Psalms* (repr., Eugene, OR: Wipf & Stock, 2006); Nancy L. deClaissé-Walford, "Embracing the Psalter's Imprecatory Words in the 21st Century," *Acta Theologica* Supplement 32 (2021): 275-92.

²Charlie Trimm, "Praying for the Peace or Destruction of Babylon? The Intersection of Enemy Love and Imprecatory Psalms in the Old Testament," *Criswell Theological Review* 17 (2020): 18-22. Trimm notes the following six elements that generally characterize imprecatory psalms: (1) a statement of innocence, (2) an acknowledgment of the psalmist's weakness, (3) a description of the actions of the evildoer, (4) a calling down of judgment on the enemy, (5) a rationale for the judgment, and (6) the goal of the judgment.

³DeClaissé-Walford, "Embracing the Psalter's Imprecatory Words," 287.

Lament and Injustice/Unfair Circumstances and Anger

of grave injustice, such as war, annihilation of people groups, extortion, oppression, and destruction of cities, which also involves torture, rape, and the killing of children. In other words, these psalms are calling out against serious evil.

Exploring various options. How are we to reconcile these harsh injunctions with Jesus' call to love our enemies and pray for them (Lk 6:27; Mt 5:44)? We are not alone in asking this question. Scholars have made several main proposals as they have wrestled with this question. First is the suggestion to view these words as simply wrong and something we should not imitate or condone. They were spoken out of human frailty. A prominent supporter of this view is C. S. Lewis, who writes, "We must not either try to explain them away or to yield for one moment to the idea that, because it comes in the Bible, all this vindictive hatred must somehow be good and pious. We must face both facts squarely. The hatred is there—festering, gloating, undisguised—and also, we should be wicked if we in any way condone or approve it."[4] Other scholars would take this perspective one step further and propose that these words were not inspired by the Holy Spirit.[5]

While it is understandable to find these words uncomfortable and seemingly contrary to other sentiments in Scripture, there are good reasons to think that the best options are not to attribute them only to the frailty of humanity or to call them uninspired. First, Psalms is the most-quoted Old Testament book in the New Testament. Jesus also quotes from the Psalms more than any other book. The imprecatory psalms are quoted at twice the average for Psalms as a whole in the New Testament.[6] Why

---

[4] C. S. Lewis, *Reflections on the Psalms* (San Diego: Harcourt, 1958), 20.

[5] "For example, Rudolf Kittel and J. Caleb Hughes write, "But there are not wanting those who, after the manner of the scribes, are superficial, or, like the mean-spirited persons who are to be found among the pious of all times, think only of rewards, or thirst after conquest and revenge. From such the notorious imprecatory psalms originated. They are a historical, instructive witness to what was at one time accredited to God. . . . To repeat them (these imprecatory psalms) would be blasphemy." Kittel and Hughes, *The Scientific Study of the Old Testament* (New York: Putnam's Sons, 1910), 143.

[6] Wenham, *The Enigma of Evil: Can We Believe in the Goodness of God?* (Grand Rapids, MI: Zondervan, 1985), 172-73. Examples of imprecatory psalm quotations in the New Testament include Jesus quoting from Ps 69 in Jn 2:17 and Peter quoting from this same psalm when choosing someone to replace Judas in Acts 1:16-20 (see Ps 69:25). In this same passage, Peter also quotes from another imprecatory psalm, Ps 109:8.

would the New Testament authors choose to quote uninspired words or words attributed to human frailty? Furthermore, Paul states in 2 Timothy 3:16 that "all" Scripture is "God-breathed" or inspired. Both the writers of the New Testament and the history of the church display the belief that Scripture in its totality is inspired and worthy of shaping its readers.

Another prominent way to reconcile these harsh words is to see them as prophetic. What this means is to see them as foretelling what will happen to the enemies of Israel, who are ultimately the enemies of God because they oppose his people. In other words, the psalmists and David are prophets foretelling both historical events and spiritual realities. David Barshinger writes about Jonathan Edwards falling into this camp. "Edwards regarded it (imprecatory language) not as personal vengeance, but as a corporate matter for the church and as prophetic of both historical events and spiritual realities within God's plan of redemption. And he tempered these observations with love for one's enemies and hope for their repentance under the gospel."[7] While certainly the psalmists were hoping for an inbreaking of God's justice in the future and indeed believed that God would be faithful to his promises, the words are more than a simple prophecy of what they believed would happen. These words express an active interaction with God, indicating the psalmists' wishes and desires in light of the current injustice.

Others think imprecatory psalms are important and should be recognized as part of the Old Testament worldview, but as New Testament believers, the teaching of Jesus has superseded this understanding. Additionally, some view the imprecatory psalms as a reflection of God's promises to Abraham and his descendants through the blessings and curses associated with them (Gen 12:1-3). More specifically, God promised to bless those who blessed his covenant people and curse those who cursed them. Therefore, it was appropriate for Israel to pray these imprecatory psalms because they are in alignment with God's promises. Carl Laney writes in this vein, "It would be inappropriate for a church-age believer to call down

---

[7]David P. Barshinger, "Spite or Spirit? Jonathan Edwards on the Imprecatory Language in the Psalms," *Westminster Theological Journal* 77, no. 1 (Spring 2015): 55.

God's judgement on the wicked. One can appreciate the Old Testament setting of the imprecatory psalms and teach and preach from them. However, like the ceremonial dietary laws of the Old Testament, the imprecations in the Psalms should not be applied to the church-age saint."[8] While it is true that there are more examples of imprecation or curses in the Old Testament than the New, there are still nonetheless examples of imprecations in the New Testament as well. For example, Jesus curses the Pharisees (Mt 23:13-39) as well as the unrepentant towns of Chorazin and Bethsaida (Mt 11:2-24). Paul curses anyone who preaches another gospel (Gal 1:8). He also curses Elymas the sorcerer in Acts 13:10-11: "You are a child of the devil and an enemy of everything that is right! You are full of all kinds of deceit and trickery. Will you never stop perverting the right ways of the Lord? Now the hand of the Lord is against you. You are going to be blind for a time, not even able to see the light of the sun." In the book of Revelation, the martyrs cry out to God for retribution on their enemies:

> When he opened the fifth seal, I saw under the altar the souls of those who had been slain because of the word of God and the testimony they had maintained. They called out in a loud voice, "How long, Sovereign Lord, holy and true, until you judge the inhabitants of the earth and avenge our blood?" Then each of them was given a white robe, and they were told to wait a little longer, until the full number of their fellow servants, their brothers and sisters, were killed just as they had been. (Rev 6:9-11)

Still another example is found in Acts 8:20-21. The word Peter uses here, *apōleianis*, is calling for annihilation, utter destruction, or eternal damnation. Second Timothy 4:14 and Acts 13:10-11 further demonstrate that notions of imprecation or cursing exist in the New Testament.

Additionally, the Old Testament is not devoid of texts that speak of loving one's neighbors or even one's enemies. This is not strictly a New Testament conception. "Do not seek revenge or bear a grudge against anyone among your people, but love your neighbor as yourself. I am the Lord" (Lev 19:18). Leviticus 19:34 states, "The foreigner residing among you must be treated as your native-born. Love them as yourself, for you

---

[8] J. Carl Laney, "A Fresh Look at the Imprecatory Psalms," *Bibliotheca Sacra* 138 (March 1981): 44.

were foreigners in Egypt. I am the LORD your God." Proverbs 25:21 notes, "If your enemy is hungry, give him food to eat; if he is thirsty, give him water to drink." Even David, who is thought to be the author of over 50 percent of the Psalms, did not deal harshly with his personal enemies when he had the chance, for example, sparing Saul twice when others urged him to kill him at the cave at En Gedi (1 Sam 24) or the Desert of Ziph (1 Sam 26:1-25) and even penning a dirge for him at his death (2 Sam 1:17-27). He also spared Shimei, who cursed him while he was fleeing Absalom (2 Sam 19:16-23). Additionally, the Psalms also speak of the psalmist mourning for his enemies (Ps 35:12-14) and extending them a hand of friendship as well as praying for them (Ps 109:4-5).[9]

Scripture indicates that it may be unwise to make too sharp a distinction between the Testaments. We can see that both the Old Testament and New Testament express both loving and calling out against enemies. And as Paul states in Galatians 3:29, "If you belong to Christ, then you are Abraham's seed, and heirs according to the promise." We do not want to make such a stark dichotomy between the promises to Abraham and to us as New Testament believers.

A balanced perspective. So what do we do? I believe that we can still pray these imprecatory psalms, but we must remember that they are part of a larger context. Trevor Laurence in his book *Cursing with God* notes that the imprecatory psalms are royal-priestly prayers, and as New Testament believers, we are sons and daughters of God, restored in Christ into our royal-priestly calling. This calling is "to tend and extend God's sanctuary dwelling, and imprecatory prayers are an exercise of that divinely granted office. Accordingly, innocently suffering Christians are to petition as priest-kings for justice against the human, systemic, and spiritual enemies of Jesus and his temple-kingdom as well as against the petitioner's and the ecclesial community's temple-corrupting sin."[10] Thus in this way the imprecatory psalms can be viewed as participating in God's plan.

---

[9]"While it is possible that the Old Testament has no theme of enemy love or that imprecatory psalms were only for times of extreme pain when it was appropriate to hate one's enemies, it is more likely that one could love an enemy while praying an imprecation against them" (Trimm, "Praying for the Peace," 33).

[10]Laurence, *Cursing with God*, 329.

Bruce Waltke has a slightly different perspective on the imprecatory psalms. He argues that they are crying out for justice, not revenge. They are grounded in the understanding of right and wrong and plead for God to do what is right. They are prayers of faith asking God to avenge rather than the psalmists taking things in their own hands. Additionally, they are written in poetic language with intentional hyperbolic and exaggerated imagery. Waltke also points out that we no longer live under a theocratic state. With these things in mind, he argues that Christians today should not pray these psalms as is. Instead, Waltke views Christians as wearing two hats.

> As Christians, we pray that God will give our enemies repentance. And yet as citizens of the state, we pray that our leaders will give us protection, maintain justice, and punish wrongdoers (Rom 13:1-4; cf. 2 Tim 2:1-12). Vengeance belongs to the Lord, and he avenges through the state. In any case, Christians must not avenge themselves (Rom 12:17-21). Like the psalmist we pray with kingdom focus, and our concern is for righteousness to triumph and for God to be honored by all.[11]

Simply put, we do not take justice into our own hands, but we leave it to the governmental authorities that God has put into place to bring justice.[12]

All this discussion of imprecatory psalms reminds us that lament is more than simply being sad about what has happened. Lament evokes a myriad of emotions within us, including anger. While contemporary Christianity has often been guilty of trying to subdue or quickly resolve anger that people experience in light of injustice, God's people have a long, rich history of expressing anger at a world not yet put to right. Imprecatory psalms are an important part of the lament process, giving honest voice to pain and anger when we witness or experience evil and

---

[11] Bruce K. Waltke and Fred G. Zaspel, *How to Read and Understand the Psalms* (Wheaton, IL: Crossway, 2023), 316.

[12] Like Waltke, Laurence notes that our imprecations should be nuanced with emphasis on repentance and reformation of one's enemies. However, he also argues that there should be room for praying imprecation, when necessary, for temporal judgment by God in order to interrupt or cease "kingdom threatening violence of the wicked by any means just and necessary." Laurence, *Cursing with God*, 274. See Laurence, *Cursing with God*, 255-326 for his thorough explanation on praying imprecation as NT believers, which I believe is helpful for us as we wrestle with these prayers.

injustice. In praying these imprecatory psalms, we express our real and valid anger and at the same time leave injustice in God's hands to handle in his good time. Imprecatory psalms allow us to lament in a way that takes injustice seriously while acknowledging the importance of letting God exact justice. Examining Psalm 94 sheds further light on this topic.

PSALM 94

> The Lord is a God who avenges.
>   O God who avenges, shine forth.
> Rise up, Judge of the earth;
>   pay back to the proud what they deserve.
> How long, Lord, will the wicked,
>   how long will the wicked be jubilant?
> They pour out arrogant words;
>   all the evildoers are full of boasting.
> They crush your people, Lord;
>   they oppress your inheritance.
> They slay the widow and the foreigner;
>   they murder the fatherless.
> They say, "The Lord does not see;
>   the God of Jacob takes no notice."
> Take notice, you senseless ones among the people;
>   you fools, when will you become wise?
> Does he who fashioned the ear not hear?
>   Does he who formed the eye not see?
> Does he who disciplines nations not punish?
>   Does he who teaches mankind lack knowledge?
> The Lord knows all human plans;
>   he knows that they are futile.
> Blessed is the one you discipline, Lord,
>   the one you teach from your law;
> you grant them relief from days of trouble,
>   till a pit is dug for the wicked.
> For the Lord will not reject his people;
>   he will never forsake his inheritance.
> Judgment will again be founded on righteousness,

Lament and Injustice/Unfair Circumstances and Anger

> and all the upright in heart will follow it.
> Who will rise up for me against the wicked?
> > Who will take a stand for me against evildoers?
> Unless the LORD had given me help,
> > I would soon have dwelt in the silence of death.
> When I said, "My foot is slipping,"
> > your unfailing love, LORD, supported me.
> When anxiety was great within me,
> > your consolation brought me joy.
> Can a corrupt throne be allied with you—
> > a throne that brings on misery by its decrees?
> The wicked band together against the righteous
> > and condemn the innocent to death.
> But the LORD has become my fortress,
> > and my God the rock in whom I take refuge.
> He will repay them for their sins
> > and destroy them for their wickedness;
> > the LORD our God will destroy them.

Recall that the following five elements are characteristic of laments. As mentioned before, not all elements will be present in every lament, and they may not follow this order.

- address or invocation
- lamentation/petition/complaint
- motivations
- confession of trust/assurance of being heard
- vow of praise

As noted above, this psalm lacks clear identification as either an individual or corporate lament psalm. Corporate or communal laments usually speak with a collective voice for the nation and are focused on concerns of the community, which are often political in nature, such as pointing out the ridicule and mockery they have received from their enemies. More specifically, these prayers usually address issues such as military defeat, war, exile, famine, drought, corruption in society, and other communal misfortunes. Additionally, communal laments often appeal to or cite God's earlier saving deeds to motivate God to intervene. They also confess trust in his deliverance and faithfulness.

Address or invocation. Psalm 94 begins by addressing God as a God of vengeance (NIV translates "God who avenges"). The Hebrew word *něqāmâ* in Psalm 94:1 refers to divine retribution, vindication, or vengeance. Here the psalmist uses this term in the plural to emphasizes how God is one who is thorough in retribution or vindication. While the concept of divine retribution or vengeance can be conceptually challenging to square with our contemporary sensibilities, it is important to remember that divine retribution and vengeance are borne out of God's holiness and justice. He cannot be truly just or good if he allows sin and rebellion to go unpunished. In the same way, a parent who ignores injustice in their household would be considered neglectful. Both the Old and New Testament have a consistent message about God's justice and vengeance. In making things new, he will indeed make all things new and punish his enemies (see, e.g., Rev 19:15).

The psalmist is purposefully addressing God as a God of vengeance because he is turning to God for justice and simultaneously asking God to champion the cause of his people. Marvin Tate views this address to God as evoking an appeal before a tribunal or court setting because the following verse refers to Yahweh as Judge of the earth (Ps 94:2).[13] In the ancient Near East, the one who judged was often also royalty or the king himself. By addressing Yahweh in this way, the psalmist is acknowledging God's rule and power to judge. The call to "shine forth" in Psalm 94:1 points back to when God appeared and manifested himself in power (see Deut 33:2-5). This is instructive because the lament begins with a clear perspective of who God is. The psalmist is not just coming to find comfort; he is coming to ask God to avenge and bring justice against the proud.

Thus the psalmist's invocation shapes his understanding of who God is and what sort of power God has to right injustice. This framing is important to remember as we face situations of injustice or anger. By

---

[13]Marvin E. Tate, *Psalms 51–100*, Word Biblical Commentary (Nashville: Thomas Nelson, 1991), 489-90.

coming to God with an understanding that God is able to right wrongs and bring forth true justice to unfair situations, we position ourselves in such a way that we can both pour out our anger and have hope that it will be heard and addressed in due time. We are not addressing a God who is impotent and unable to do anything about the evil we see happening all around us. We are coming before the King of kings and the Judge of the earth. Our perspective needs to begin here when we are lamenting situations of injustice.

In the New Testament, Jesus tells the story of the persistent widow who comes continually comes before an unjust judge (Lk 18:1-18). This unjust judge finally grants the widow her justice so that she will not eventually wear him down (Lk 18:4). Jesus is not calling us to pray because God is an unjust judge who needs to be worn down. No, he is telling us that if persistence can wear down an unjust judge, how much more our just Heavenly Father, who cares for his people (Lk 18:7-8). God is able and willing to deal with the injustices we bring before him. Let us come before him with faith, trusting that he is our Judge and a God of vindication.

Lamentation/petition/complaint. The psalmist then moves in the next five verses (Ps 94:3-7) to lamenting the wickedness and recounting the distress that surrounds him. Notice that Psalm 94:3 begins with two very honest questions: "How long, Lord, will the wicked, how long will the wicked be jubilant?" Again, these are rhetorical questions that are simultaneously stating that it has been far too long while as the same time asking for God to act. The wicked are rejoicing in their success over crushing the faithful followers of God (Ps 94:5) and even murdering the weak, for example, widows, orphans, and sojourners (Ps 94:6). The psalmist does not mince words. He is telling God that this is wrong and asking God to arise (Ps 94:2) and do something because these wicked ones think that God does not see (Ps 94:7). They think they are above the law, that no one is going to hold them accountable.

While we sometimes feel like the words of imprecatory psalms are harsh, it is easy from the comfort of our modern Western society to forget the sheer evil that exists in the world. I was reminded of this when I watched a documentary on a serial killer who showed no remorse for his deeds but taunted the family members of his victims by calling them with the deceased victim's old cellphone and even bragged smugly about how the police were unable to catch their killer. This story is shocking to the senses because it exemplifies the utterly inhumane evil that is prevalent in the world. Perhaps this was the kind of unbearable evil that the psalmist witnessed when he spoke about these murderers and perpetrators of social injustice.

Notice, too, that while the psalmist is not necessarily stating that the offense is personal, it is safe to say that he identifies with those who are called God's people (Ps 94:5). This leaves the psalm open-ended in terms of applying to situations that are personal versus corporate. In fact, the psalm shows a vacillation between forms that are third-person plural (corporate; Ps 94:3-11), first-person singular (individual; Ps 94:16-22), and first-person plural (corporate, Ps 94:23). The third-person reference to oppression and desire of justice continues through Psalm 94:15, but later in the psalm we see a first-person "I" and "my" point of view describing his struggle in Psalm 94:16-22. It then reverts back to the corporate "we" in the last verse (Ps 94:23). Noticing these grammar shifts is instructive because situations of injustice and evil can touch us individually and simultaneously affect us corporately.

As mentioned earlier, the psalm is not speaking about minor infractions; imprecatory psalms are dealing with situations of grave injustice. When we experience or face situations that are unjust, we can bring our anger before the Lord and lay it down before his throne. We can recount what we see and how evil seems to be prevailing against us individually and corporately. We can express our desire for justice and the anger that wells in our hearts because of our outrage at oppression that is taking place. The psalmist sets an example for us. He does not whitewash the situation or make it less than it is. He is honest, and we can be too. He is also not only speaking for himself, but is advocating for justice for his community. When we acknowledge that injustice and evil are prevalent, we do not have to give into feelings of defeat or apathy. Like the psalmist, let us bring our feelings of anger and desire for justice before our just and powerful King.

Motivations. Psalm 94:3-7 offers multiple reasons why God should act. First, the psalmist mentions people groups he knows will get God's attention, namely, God's people and those who are marginalized, for example, widows, orphans, and sojourners. Have you ever seen a mama bear step into action when she thinks her cubs are being threatened? Hopefully not! It would not be pretty, and you would not come out unscathed. By recounting to God how the wicked are crushing his people and murdering the helpless (Ps 94:5-6), the psalmist is appealing to God's protective nature as a father as well as his role as the defender of the defenseless. Repeatedly in Scripture, God is characterized as one who cares for the oppressed (Ex 22:22-23; Deut 10:18; 24:19; Ps 68:5; 146:9; Is 10:1-34; Mal 3:5). God's people and those who need his help are being crushed and killed—and as a result, the enemies are not just those of God's people, but they have become God's enemies. You may know the saying, "If you mess with my child (or family, friends, etc.), you are messing with me." The psalmist is basically telling God that the wicked are messing with God's people and therefore they are really messing with God.

The second motivation the psalmist gives is that these evil ones are proud (Ps 94:2) and exult over their wickedness (Ps 94:3). They even speak defiantly against God (Ps 94:7) and his ability to see and deal with injustice. They are speaking with arrogance and distain toward Yahweh's willingness or ability to intervene. The psalmist is appealing to the justice of God. How can God allow this to continue?

Like the psalmist, we have in our minds thresholds that we think should not be crossed pertaining to justice and evil that should not be tolerated. We do not have to relax our standards so that we can tolerate injustice. We can offer motivations for God to act through our prayers. Like Habakkuk, who voiced questions based on the incongruency he saw between God's justice and the use of wicked people as instruments of justice, we can also use our struggles to motivate God to action. We can be like the widow with the unjust judge, coming persistently before God. We do not have to give way to apathy or indifference. We can name the evil and ask God to act.

Confession of trust/assurance of being heard. While the shift from lament to hope is often indicated by the conjunctions "but" or "now" (e.g., Ps 55:16, 23), in this psalm the poem shifts to a different audience. Instead of addressing Yahweh, the psalmist shifts his attention to "the senseless ones" and "fools" (Ps 94:8), who in the context of this psalm are the same as the "wicked" (Ps 94:3) and "evildoers" (Ps 94:4) mentioned earlier. These are the ones who boast, "The Lord does not see; the God of Jacob takes no notice" (Ps 94:7). The psalmist confronts their arrogance with a rebuttal in the form of three consecutive rhetorical questions grounded in creation and world history:

> Does he who fashioned the ear not hear?
>   Does he who formed the eye not see?
> Does he who disciplines nations not punish? (Ps 94:9-10a)

In the second half of Psalm 94:10, the psalmist transitions to the objective of these rhetorical questions, going on to say in Psalm 94:11, "The Lord knows the thoughts of man, that they are but a breath" (ESV). This statement highlights God's universal knowledge and compares it to the transitory nature of humanity's thoughts. The word for "breath" is the Hebrew word *hebel*, "meaningless," which is continually repeated in the book of Ecclesiastes to refer to the absurdity or transitory nature of life (see Eccles 1:1). The psalmist is confronting the wicked with the reality of God and acknowledging God's sovereignty as the universal judge over humanity's insignificance.

He then transitions in Psalm 94:12-15 with words of confident assurance of being heard.

> Blessed is the one you discipline, Lord,
>   the one you teach from your law;
> you grant them relief from days of trouble,
>   till a pit is dug for the wicked.
> For the Lord will not reject his people;
>   he will never forsake his inheritance.
> Judgment will again be founded on righteousness,
>   and all the upright in heart will follow it.

Through these statements the psalmist is not only asserting his confidence in God's justice and faithfulness, but he is also encouraging those who are trying to be faithful (Ps 94:12-13). These words of blessing are common to Wisdom literature (Ps 1:1-3; Prov 3:13-17; 8:32-36). In English they are referred to as words of beatitude (Mt 5:3-12). The psalmist is assuring those whom the Lord disciplines and who receive teaching from his law that they will not be forsaken. The wicked ones will receive their just punishment in the pit that is dug for them (Ps 94:13). The pit in this context is referring to how these proud evildoers will eventually receive their just recompense (see Prov 26:27). In the same way, the God of justice will turn or bring back justice to the righteous (Ps 94:15).

In this section the psalmist is declaring God's faithfulness to his people and acknowledging that those who seek the Lord will find rest from trouble because the Lord will not forsake them (Ps 94:14). He will bring about justice to the righteous (Ps 94:15). Even though the lament began by imploring God to action, the psalmist is reassuring himself and others that God is faithful. This public declaration is mostly based on the psalmist's following personal experience.

Vow of praise. The final section (Ps 94:16-23) contains continued statements of assurance based on the psalmist's own experience of deliverance. It is closely associated with the previous assurance of being heard and confession of trust. His personal experience of God's faithfulness (Ps 94:16-19) results in praise for God as his rock and refuge (Ps 94:22). But rather than offering a future vow of praise, this section provides a present statement of praise. The psalmist begins with two rhetorical questions that everyone, including the reader, knows the answer to (Ps 94:16-17).

> Who will rise up for me against the wicked?
> Who will take a stand for me against evildoers?
> Unless the Lord have given me help,
> I would soon have dwelt in the silence of death.

The poet uses the metaphor of the psalmist's foot almost slipping (Ps 94:18) to describe a close call. Was this close call an actual physical threat, or is it intended to refer to a loss of faith? Marvin Tate argues that Psalm 94:19 suggests that Psalm 94:18 indicates a near collapse in the psalmist's faith (see Ps 73:2), while others, such as Dennis Tucker, argue that it was an extreme situation when he was close to physical death (see Ps 94:17).[14] Whatever the case, God's steadfast love or *ḥesed* sustained him (Ps 94:18). When evil and injustice surround us, we must focus on God's *ḥesed*, his faithful lovingkindness and mercy. Recall that this term refers to God's eternal loyal lovingkindness that is closely associated with the covenant relationship he has with his people (Ex 20; Deut 5). Moreover, this type of love is actualized through action, as this word is often used with action verbs such as "show," "do," or "keep" (Ruth 1:8-9; Josh 2:12). God's *ḥesed* is also used in contexts where one party is helping another that is in need, hence the translation "mercy." This love brought the psalmist back from the brink of death or losing his faith.

The psalmist also received divine comfort in his inner being or soul. This word for comfort, *tanḥûm* ("comforts/consolations"), is used elsewhere in the context of the face of death (see Jer 16:7; Is 66:11, where it describes the comforting breasts of a mother). The word can also refer to the relief of emotional stress and grief as well as the satisfaction of the mind. Here the psalmist describes how God's consolations gladden his soul or inner being. God can bring comfort even in the midst of injustice and evil. Similarly, we can experience God as our defense, rock, and refuge (Ps 94:22) when we are facing grave injustice.

As we have noted in other psalms, the psalmist circles back and raises another rhetorical question, here with the Hebrew interrogative *hă*. Questions using this interrogative are usually rhetorical and expect a negative answer. "When *hă* appears in a question that question is not asking primarily for information but rather is a rhetorical question to which usually a negative answer is expected ('Am I my brother's keeper?' Gen 4:9) and occasionally a positive answer."[15] The psalmist is affirming in his question that God is a God of justice, and he is not in alliance with the wicked, who gather against the righteous and condemn the innocent (Ps 94:21). While these situations of injustice continue to

---

[14]Tate, *Psalms 51–100*, 459; W. Dennis Tucker Jr. and Jamie A. Grant, *Psalms*, vol. 2, NIV Application Commentary (Grand Rapids, MI: Zondervan Academic, 2018), 394.

[15]Victor P. Hamilton, "ה," in *Theological Wordbook of the Old Testament*, ed. R. Laird Harris, Gleason L. Archer Jr., and Bruce K. Waltke (Chicago: Moody Press, 1980), 1:204.

plague the psalmist's mind, he is still able to declare that God is just. This is why he can firmly praise God in Psalm 94:22 and confidently know that the wicked will face destruction (Ps 94:23). Tate writes, "The Judge of the Earth, who dispenses discipline to nations, will not long tolerate the vaunting pride of the evildoers and their 'seat of destruction.' Yahweh is a 'turn-backer' of judgment onto the wicked and of justice onto the righteous (v 15)."[16]

Psalm 94 reflects the journey of one who is wrestling with injustice to the point of almost losing his faith (Ps 94:18), but God's lovingkindness and sovereignty provide the anchor he needs for his soul. He is able to honestly bring his complaints and doubts to the Judge of all the earth. Leaving the situation before God and trusting that God will vindicate frees the psalmist to declare hope not only to himself but to others. God's faithfulness and his consolations can free us to act without bitterness. The Lord will bring about vengeance and recompense. We do not have to carry the heavy burden of enacting justice on our own. After all, only God can right wrongs and bring justice to the righteous (Ps 94:15) while justly returning destruction back on the wicked (Ps 94:23). Ingrid's story shows God's faithfulness in a situation of injustice.

Ingrid's Story

For fifteen years, I steadily built my business with integrity, developing products to help self-employed and small business owners through large national insurance carriers. I tithed faithfully, gave freely, and sought to build good relationships with my staff, agents, clients, and vendors. My business grew to a thousand agents selling our products, with 350 being paid commissions in the Chicagoland area alone. My titles included wife, mother, entrepreneur, business owner, friend, and director of women's ministries at my local church, and I had just added the role of student in a master of divinity program.

With this last addition of student, I entrusted more of my business operations to the person who had worked with me for seven years.

---

[16] Tate, *Psalms 51–100*, 495.

Foolishly, this included bank signing privileges on our client premium trust fund accounts. At this point my husband had already been sick and disabled for seven years with severe, constant pain. His mounting health problems began with dental malpractice, which led to sepsis and most excruciatingly chronic pancreatitis. Daily we sought to manage his pain while I was running my businesses and household.

I began taking classes in divinity school because I was seeking to understand where God was in the hardships my husband and I (and so many others) experienced. What I did not expect was for my trusted and well-paid right-hand person to start taking monies for personal needs and home remodeling out of our clients' premium trust fund accounts. With my husband's deteriorating health over the next two years, I did not discover the steadily missing funds until near the time of my husband's death. This employee, whom I had considered a trusted friend, had prepared for this moment with one of my competitors. As soon as I began to ask questions, they transferred our client database to my competitor, contacted all my clients to now do business with the new entity, and told my attorney and questioning clients that I was unavailable due to a nervous breakdown, which was entirely false.

With a domino effect of consequences amid this perfect storm, I financially lost everything I had ever earned, saved, or invested. A judge (presumed friend of my competitor) closed the case and then retired, leaving me without recourse. Within a short time, most of my relationships, titles, identity, and resources had dissolved. Even many people at church distanced themselves from me, presuming I must have sinned for so many hardships to have fallen on me.

For several months, the only Bible verse I could muster reading was the opening of Psalm 22, "My God, my God, why have you forsaken me? Why are you so far from helping me, from the words of my groaning? O my God, I cry by day, but you do not answer; and by night, but find no rest" (Ps 22:1-2 NRSV). Yet, even as I read this, I knew the rest of the psalm, that it ended in praise and ultimately with the resurrection after Jesus quoted those words. For a long season, the Psalms were my only solace. As I read Psalm 41:9, "Even my bosom friend in whom I trusted, who ate of my bread, has lifted the heel against me" (NRSV), I realized that Jesus chose Judas, knowing he would be betrayed, so that he as my high priest could bear my burden and feel my sorrow. As I read Psalm 69:1-3, "Save me, O God, for the waters have come up to my neck. I sink in deep mire, where there is no foothold; I have come into deep waters, and the flood sweeps over me. I am weary with my crying; my throat is parched. My eyes grow dim with waiting for my God" (NRSV), cries of anguish and loss mingled with hope in God. The growing anger was met with the assurance that God sees and that God would act. Knowing that the Judge of the earth will do justice (Gen 18:25) helped me to gradually release my resentment and desire for retribution, knowing that justice would be meted out either in this life or after and God would handle it better than I would.

The lament and imprecatory psalms gave me language to express my hurt and rage and also gave me the assurance that I was seen. Evil would be dealt with by the only one capable of doing it equitably. The antidote to the poison of hatred and unforgiveness toward the people and systems that failed me was trust in the only one who could, and who did, bear it all himself.

In the years that have ensued, I have seen the goodness of God prevail in my life. I am deeply thankful that I never gave up on God or on living, although I considered those options for a season. But God spoke to my heart with Psalm 23:4, "Even though I walk through the darkest valley, I fear no evil; for you are with me" (NRSV), and pointed out that I was not to lie down in the valley of the shadow of death. I was not to set up camp there. Rather, I was to fear nothing bad and walk through each one because God was with me. Since then, I have experienced miracles of all kinds and have grown to trust God's justice and goodness. Even when troubles and challenges assail, and they do, I can be honest and say that I do not like them. But I am also honest when I say I am not afraid and I am not going to take them lying down, because God is with me to walk through them, and I expect good ahead. My life has become rich in satisfaction, abundant in love and friendships, and filled with the presence of God. I only wish I was taught about the purpose and process of lament as a young Christian.

REFLECTION QUESTIONS

1. What are the various views on the imprecatory psalms? Do you think we can pray these psalms as Christians today? Why or why not?
2. Are you dealing with issues of injustice in your own life?
3. How does lament help us to avoid the extremes of apathy and the desire to take revenge?
4. How can lament help us to move forward even when we have experienced injustice?

INDIVIDUAL PRACTICE

Is there some injustice that you have been experiencing or carrying in your heart? Allow yourself the freedom to express your honest feelings before the Lord, even if it feels unsettling. Sometimes we hold back for fear of being struck down by lightning if we were to express what we truly feel. If you are angry, let God know, journal, cry, yell, ask him for the justice you need in your situation. Reread Psalm 94 and meditate on the verses that stand out to you. Wait in silence and ask the Lord for renewed strength and perspective in your situation.

CORPORATE PRACTICE

Spend some time in your church service acknowledging that all is not right in the world. If necessary, list and name the injustices that you hear on the news and that are prevalent in your community. Invite those carrying burdens or experiencing injustice to pray. Be sure to also give room for silence so others' concerns and words can be heard. Read Psalm 94 together and pray for the situations shared.

8

Lament and Loneliness/Abandonment

A 2021 study from Harvard reports that more than one-third of Americans (36 percent) feel serious loneliness, which means they frequently feel lonely or feel lonely almost all the time or all the time. The study indicates that to one degree or another, loneliness has plagued most Americans. In addition to the 36 percent who experience serious loneliness, an additional 37 percent of respondents who reported feeling lonely occasionally. The study also found that loneliness was pervasive across all major demographic groups. "Among our survey respondents, there were no significant differences in rates of loneliness based on race or ethnicity, gender, level of education, income, religion, or urbanicity."[1] While the worldwide pandemic heightened these numbers, loneliness has been consistently on the rise for decades. This has implications not only for individual mental health but also for the nation at large. Vivek Murthy, who served as the nineteenth surgeon general of the United States (2014–2017), calls loneliness an epidemic that not only affects individual mental health but also workplace productivity to the tune of $154 billion annually.[2]

---

[1] Richard Weissbourd, Milena Batanova, Virginia Lovison, and Eric Torres, "Loneliness in America: How the Pandemic Has Deepened an Epidemic of Loneliness and What We Can Do About It," Making Caring Common, 2021, https://static1.squarespace.com/static/5b7c56e255b02c683659fe43/t/6021776bdd04957c4557c212/1612805995893/Loneliness+in+America+2021_02_08_FINAL.pdf.

[2] Vivek Murthy, "Work and the Loneliness Epidemic," *Harvard Business Review*, September 26, 2017, https://hbr.org/2017/09/work-and-the-loneliness-epidemic.

All of us face times of loneliness in life. We can be in a crowded room and feel alone, or we can be facing circumstances that leave us feeling unsupported and vulnerable. If we live life long enough, most of us will experience at least one season of loneliness. Scripture tells us that even Jesus experienced loneliness when his disciples, whom he had poured into for three years, fled and left him during his greatest time of need. He was left to face the journey to the cross on his own. I am sure the abandonment and betrayal he experienced only compounded his feelings of loneliness. After all, it was one of his twelve disciples who betrayed him with a kiss.

Though everyone experiences feelings of loneliness, there are times when these feelings seem especially difficult. How can we walk through this season with the Lord? How can the process of lament be instructive for us?

While there are several individual lament psalms that speak of loneliness and struggle, I find Psalms 42–43 to be especially helpful. These psalms are often viewed as a unit because they share the same themes, and both repeat a refrain that is almost word for word in Psalm 42:5, 11 [6, 12] and Psalm 43:5. Several ancient manuscripts also present these two psalms as one. Both are psalms of individual lament that give voice to the struggle with feelings of loneliness and abandonment, not only by others but also by God. Often our struggle with loneliness includes feelings of distance from God. We wonder whether he even sees our sadness and pain. At these times, like the psalmist, our struggle is intensified by questions about the existence or nearness of God's presence (see Ps 42:3, 10 [4, 11]). Some commentators believe that these two psalms were written in the context of Jerusalem's destruction and Judah's exile because of the psalmist's struggles with abandonment by God. However, these psalms do not provide enough specific details to prove this to be true. What is clear is that the psalmist is dealing with feelings of loneliness. Instead of looking for specifics surrounding the psalmist's hardship, highlighting the general nature makes the psalm more applicable to any circumstance. Clearly, there is a struggle within the psalmist's heart. He desires to come before God but also mourns his current situation. Let us take a closer look at these psalms.

Lament and Loneliness/Abandonment

PSALMS 42 AND 43

Psalm 42
As the deer pants for streams of water,
    so my soul pants for you, my God.
My soul thirsts for God, for the living God.
    When can I go and meet with God?
My tears have been my food
    day and night,
while people say to me all day long,
    "Where is your God?"
These things I remember
    as I pour out my soul:
how I used to go to the house of God
    under the protection of the Mighty One
with shouts of joy and praise
    among the festive throng.
Why, my soul, are you downcast?
    Why so disturbed within me?
Put your hope in God,
    for I will yet praise him,
    my Savior and my God.
My soul is downcast within me;
    therefore I will remember you
from the land of the Jordan,
    the heights of Hermon—from Mount Mizar.
Deep calls to deep
    in the roar of your waterfalls;
all your waves and breakers
    have swept over me.
By day the LORD directs his love,
    at night his song is with me—
    a prayer to the God of my life.
I say to God my Rock,
    "Why have you forgotten me?
Why must I go about mourning,
    oppressed by the enemy?"

My bones suffer mortal agony
    as my foes taunt me,
saying to me all day long,
    "Where is your God?"
Why, my soul, are you downcast?
    Why so disturbed within me?
Put your hope in God,
    for I will yet praise him,
    my Savior and my God.

Psalm 43

Vindicate me, my God,
    and plead my cause
    against an unfaithful nation.
Rescue me from those who are
    deceitful and wicked.
You are God my stronghold.
    Why have you rejected me?
Why must I go about mourning,
    oppressed by the enemy?
Send me your light and your faithful care,
    let them lead me;
let them bring me to your holy mountain,
    to the place where you dwell.
Then I will go to the altar of God,
    to God, my joy and my delight.
I will praise you with the lyre,
    O God, my God.
Why, my soul, are you downcast?
    Why so disturbed within me?
Put your hope in God,
    for I will yet praise him,
    my Savior and my God.

Recall that the following five elements are characteristic of laments. As mentioned before, not all elements will be present in every lament, and they may not follow this order.

Lament and Loneliness/Abandonment

- address or invocation
- lamentation/petition/complaint
- motivations
- confession of trust/assurance of being heard
- vow of praise

Address or invocation. The psalmist begins by addressing God through the vocative *Elohim* rather than *Yahweh*, which is characteristic of the psalms in book two of the Psalter.[3] What stands out about this address is the usage of imagery through a simile to expresses the psalmist's desire to be with God. This simile compares his desire for God to thirst. More specifically, it likens his thirst to that of a deer that pants for flowing streams. This image expresses desperation. A deer that pants is not only thirsty but overheating. This is not a pretty picture. The deer is not quietly or gracefully looking for water. If it is a really hot day, a panting deer will have its tongue out to cool down. Unlike humans, who sweat when they are overheating, deer pant to excrete body heat. If you have become seriously overheated, you know that it is accompanied by exhaustion, faintness, fatigue, and dehydration. In extreme cases it results in the shutdown of vital organs and can even lead to death. The psalmist is painting a picture of desperation. More specifically, he is showing how he desires to turn to God in his time of desperation. He knows that God is the only one who can help him. As we see later in the psalm, this desperate cry is expressing loneliness, pain from abandonment, weakness, and despair in his soul.

Lamentation/petition/complaint. Before discussing the specifics of lamentation, petition, and complaint in these two psalms, I want to highlight that these psalms exhibit an alternation between despair and hope, which is a realistic picture for those dealing with feelings of loneliness and abandonment. Lament is a process. It does not always follow a consistent upward trajectory. There are moments when we feel more hopeful, but

---

[3]There are five books in the book of Psalms: book 1, Ps 1–41; book 2, Ps 42–72; book 3, Ps 73–89; book 4, Ps 90–106; book 5, Ps 107–150. The psalms in book 2 contain more psalms that use the word *Elohim* to address God.

there are also moments when despair gets the best of us. These two psalms reflect this alternating shift in emotions.

Psalms 42–43 presents a man who is wrestling with his desire to come before God but feeling alone and abandoned (Ps 42:2-3 [3-4]). The Hebrew is literally "to appear before the face of God." This imagery often refers to coming before God in his temple, which is more explicitly stated in Psalm 43:3-4. Coming before God in his temple also points to the psalmist's presence within the community, enjoying God's presence with others (Ps 42:4 [5]). He contrasts his past with how he is now alone and away from his community as well as from God.

His tears have been his food day and night. This literary expression paints a picture of mourning that is all-encompassing. The psalmist is expressing how his whole being has been swallowed up by grief. Those who experience such deep grief do not eat because they are consumed by sorrow. Often when I experience mild anxiety or grief, I turn to food as a comfort, but when I went through the painful situation of my divorce, my appetite was gone. I was so devastated that I could not eat or sleep for two weeks, and I lost over twenty pounds in that short period. Like the psalmist, my feelings of abandonment and loneliness left me disorientated and full of sorrow. Tears became my sustenance because food was repulsive to me.

The psalmist not only experiences deep sorrow but is taunted by the question of God's absence in the midst of his pain (Ps 42:3 [4]). Unlike in Psalm 42:10 [11], the Hebrew in this verse does not name an explicit subject who raises this question. While English translations add "people" or "they" to Psalm 42:3 [4], the Hebrew does not have an explicit subject for the infinitive verb "to say." Seen in this way, the sorrow that the psalmist experiences could be exacerbated by his own internal question of God's absence, plaguing him internally as he weeps day and night. Often when we feel alone and abandoned by people, we wonder about God's presence as well. Our loneliness may even be heightened because we feel that God is also absent.

The psalmist then proceeds to recall better days in the past. He recalls times when he led the people of God in shouts of rejoicing and songs of praise during the festival celebrations (Ps 42:4 [5]). This remembrance prompts him to speak to his own soul (Ps 42:[6]), which is a refrain that is repeated several more times in these two psalms. Suffering can cause us to long for past times that were more pleasant. However, instead of sinking further into his depression when he remembers the past, the psalmist speaks to his own soul. This is the first time we see the alternation between despair and a desire to move forward.

After the refrain and a brief exhortation, the psalmist returns to his lamentation in Psalm 42:7 [8]. He presents further imagery that deals with water. This time, instead of thirst or endless tears, he describes his feeling of being overwhelmed by sorrow with an image of the deep sea. While the deep sea in the Psalms often points to primordial images of chaos, an aspect that is present here as well, the phrase "deep calls to deep" could also be expressing how the psalmist calls out to the only one who understands the depth of his pain. Loneliness causes us to long for a depth of understanding from others. When we experience an abyss of pain in our hearts, we reach out to the only one who is deep enough to fill it.

The psalmist then continues to describe imagery of floods of water or waterfalls and surging waves. These can be interpreted as the psalmist feeling like waves and breakers are sweeping over him. If you have ever experienced large waves in the ocean, it can be overwhelming and even scary because you do not know when you will be able to break through the surface to catch your breath. You have no footing, and the waves keep coming and passing over your head. Likewise, deep emotional pain and sorrow can manifest in physical feelings of breathlessness or palpations that leave us longing to catch our breath. Other times intense crying can also leave us breathless as well. These images paint a picture of one who is acknowledging real feelings. The psalmist is not trying to avoid them but facing them head-on, even though it is not easy. Perhaps the hardest thing about lament is working through these painful feelings instead of quickly moving past them. If I am honest, I do not want to deal with these difficult raw emotions. I would rather move forward and press on. However, like with any physical injury, we need to endure the pain that accompanies the healing. Similarly, we cannot just paint over a wall when there are underlying mold or mildew issues. The paint can cover up for a time, but the real issues will eventually bleed through.

After a brief affirmation of God's love, the psalmist continues to question why God has forgotten him in Psalm 42:9 [10] as he mourns under the oppression of his enemies. This is the first time in the psalm that he speaks of his enemies. Similar phrasing and questions are repeated later in Psalm 43:2. These verses form a frame around his experience with his enemies. This is significant because God's absence and our loneliness are felt more acutely in the presence of haters. When we do not have someone on our side, we feel even more isolated.

The psalmist then describes how he feels his suffering down to his very bones. This image coupled with verbal taunts offers an even more graphic picture of the agony he feels (Ps 42:10 [11]). The psalmist repeats the earlier refrain to his soul (Ps 42:11 [12]). As noted earlier, these two psalms vacillate between mourning and desire for hope. The psalmist moves from longing to be in God's presence, including with his community, to feeling abandoned and rejected by God in the mist of his enemies.

As the prayer continues into Psalm 43, the psalmist makes known his desire for an advocate (Ps 43:1). He longs for God to vindicate and plead his case against the ungodly. He also asks for deliverance from deceitful and wicked ones. While he acknowledges God as his stronghold, he again vacillates as he did in Psalm 42:9 [10] and uses similar wording to question God's abandonment of him as he mourns under the oppression of his enemies. However, instead of wallowing in his pain, he continues to petition God to send his light and truth or faithfulness to lead him to God's holy mountain. This petition is important because it shows that the psalmist knows that it is only in God's presence that he will find the peace he truly desires.

Motivations. As in previous psalms, the reasons given for God to act or move are primarily rooted in God's character, as indicated in the psalmist's requests for vindication. He asks for God to act because his enemies are deceitful and unjust (Ps 43:1-2). He also appeals to his intimate relationship with God. In the midst of his struggles and doubts, he continues to refer to God as his God (Ps 42:1, 5, 8-9, 11; 43:1-2, 4-5), his "stronghold" (Ps 43:3) his "salvation" (Ps 42:5, 11; 43:5) his rock (Ps 42:9), and his exceeding joy (Ps 43:4).[4] He also appeals to God as the one who saves and protects him because recognizes his helplessness before his enemies and calls on the one he trusts in. Even in his doubts and feelings of distance from God's presence, he is still acknowledging the reality of the relationship he has with the Lord. He is remembering in the dark what he has seen in the light. This is an important aspect in lament because we can easily lose sight of reality when our emotions get the best of us. Darkness and loneliness can sometimes color our vision such that we cannot see beyond the feelings we are experiencing at the moment. At these times we need to pray because we know that God is still our God, even when we feel like he has forgotten us. The psalmist exemplifies this well in his prayer. Even though he doubts, he does not forsake what he knows to be true about God and his relationship with God.

Confession of trust/assurance of being heard. Unlike other psalms that show a starker transition from despair to assurance of being heard or a confession of trust, this psalm vacillates between depression and confessions of trust. The most obvious confessions of trust are seen in the repeated refrain in Psalm 42:5, 11 [6, 12] and Psalm 43:5.

> Why, my soul, are you downcast?
>   Why so disturbed within me?
> Put your hope in God;
>   for I will yet praise him,
>   my Savior and my God.

The psalmist speaks to his own soul, encouraging himself to hope or wait on the Lord because he affirms that he will praise God, who is his savior. The transition is indicated through the conjunction translated "because/for." In this context, this Hebrew word *kî* marks a shift from lament to hope. The psalmist is encouraging himself to hope and wait on the Lord.

This refrain models how we can speak to our own souls. Perhaps there is no one around you to speak words of hope or encouragement. It is

---

[4] The Hebrew in Ps 42:5 [6] is literally "the salvation of my face," also in Ps 42:11; 43:5. Perhaps the psalmist chose this because he speaks of his desire to appear before God, literally the "face of God," in Ps 42:2 [3].

precisely at these times when we need to speak to our own souls. We need to encourage ourselves with what we know to be true about God and his faithfulness. Being alone does not mean that we must give way to voices of despair and desolation. We can still speak hope in contrast to those voices. It is easy to give way in such a situation because the voice of self-pity is reinforced when we feel like we have no one who cares for us. Additionally, the devil, our adversary, capitalizes on these opportunities by adding more voices to this cacophony of hopelessness. However, this is exactly when we need to fight against these thoughts and voices. We must be like the psalmist, speaking to our souls. We must wield our only offensive weapon, the sword of the spirit, which is the word of God (Eph 6:17). We must remind ourselves of the truth found in God's word, namely that God saves. He can deliver us from our despair and loneliness. The present does not define our future. Moreover, as New Testament believers we have an even greater hope than the psalmist. Jesus has already delivered us from our greatest enemies, namely, sin and death. Romans 8:35-39 tells us that there is now nothing that can separate us from God's love. He who did not spare his own Son will not abandon us now. Jesus faced abandonment from the Father so that we do not have to. Like the psalmist, we need to speak truth and hope into our situations of hopelessness and despair.

Also interesting about this refrain is that the psalmist is not merely speaking to his own soul; rather, he *commands* his soul to hope or wait on God. The Hebrew verb for hoping or waiting here is a command or an imperative form. It is not a suggestion among several options, not a wish or a statement but a command. This is an important reminder that when we speak truth, it is not a suggestion. We must even command our own souls when we do not feel like it.

I know that when I am depressed or lonely, the last thing I want to do is obey. I would rather wallow in my sadness or despair, but here the psalmist is speaking another voice into the despair he has been voicing to God. The process of lament is exactly that, a process. We can acknowledge our pain and longings before God, but there will come a time that we need to also command our souls to heed the truth of Scripture. We need to desire to move forward and put our gaze on what God has promised and continues to promise for us as his children. The Hebrew term *yāḥal* ("to wait"), which is used in this refrain, also means "to hope." We are not just passively sitting around wallowing in our emotions. No, we are actively hoping and trusting that God will come through, with *active* hope and trust. Practically speaking, this means we are going to move forward in faith by putting one foot in front of the other. We are going to do what God has given us to do with faithfulness, trusting that God will bring about the change we are hoping for. We are going to wash our faces, put on our clothes, go out for a walk, call that friend, serve in that ministry, and put our eyes forward to engage others even in the midst of our own pain.

Vow of praise. The vow of praise in these psalms is found most obviously in Psalm 43:4, where the psalmist states that he will come before the altar of God, who is his joy and delight, to praise him. This vow is predicated on God's sending his light and truth to lead the psalmist into God's presence. The psalmist not only vows to let God's light and care to lead him to God (Ps 43:3) but also says when that he comes before God, he will praise him. Again, this is a future orientation. The psalmist looks forward in expectation for a time when he will offer up praises to God.

It is important to note that this is not the final word in the psalm. The repeated refrain ends the psalm. This only reinforces how our emotions are fickle. Even though we can be filled with hope in one moment, we must continue to speak to our souls because we can easily give way to despair. When we lament through such difficulties, we are facing them with honesty and truth. Elise's story shows what it looks like to lament before God when we are overwhelmed with loneliness.

Elise's Story

I lost everything when my children and I were abandoned by my husband. I was the loneliest I had ever been in my life. I had lost so much weight and looked so physically feeble that my mother told me I looked like I had HIV/AIDS. I was depending on the Lord for every breath. During this time of lament, I did not see any end in sight, nor could I conceive how I would come out alive. There was no understanding that I could endure this time and come out thriving. But we serve a God who loves to make the impossible possible, and it was through my lament that I experienced healing and the ability to flourish.

My process of recovery was not an easy one. There were layers that I had to recover from, which included a physical, mental, and spiritual restoration. The Lord met me in each layer to transform me. I daily submitted my physical, mental, and spiritual health to him. During those times, Isaiah 64:4-5 spoke to me. "[God] *acts* for those who wait for Him. You *meet* him who joyfully works righteousness, those who remember you in your ways" (ESV).

Because of the trauma I endured, there were several physical consequences. I could not eat, and I was literally starving myself because I could not get any food down. I remember one night when my five-year-old daughter was sick and lying in bed with me. She was feverish and moaning, crying for medicine. I got out of bed to get her more medicine and woke up lying on the floor with her above me and blood on the floor. She was crying, "Mommy, mommy, are you okay?" I had passed out when I got up to get her medicine and fell on the floor, cutting my hand as I fell. I was physically destitute during this time, and until I could heal physically, I was not able to fully change mentally and spiritually. I needed medication to help with the anxiety and panic attacks so that I could eat and gain my physical strength.

Through time I recovered physically. I was an athlete and had exercised my entire life. I had even run a marathon, so getting back into exercise was crucial for obtaining the physical and mental health I needed. I also had very good counselors and therapists who were helping my children and me through the grieving process. Along with this, I was daily looking to God for peace and hope as I lamented before him.

I clung to verses from Scripture and claimed them as promises from heaven. I had several promises that I meditated on each day: Psalm 68:6, "God places the lonely in families" (NLT); Isaiah 26:3, "You keep [her] in perfect peace whose mind is stayed on you, because [she] trusts in you" (ESV); Isaiah 40:11, "He gently leads those that have young" (NIV); and 1 Peter 5:6,

"Humble yourselves, therefore, under the mighty hand of God, so that in due time he may exalt you" (NET note on "mighty hand" for 1 Pet 5:6).

I am an extrovert, so it was a daily process to lament in my loneliness and trust that God would get me through the despair I felt in isolation. I had to look to God for intimacy because I have chosen to not look for it in another person while I am raising my children. I still long to be married and hope that I can meet someone when my children go to college, but until that time, I continue to practice lament in this area of my life.

The practice of lament also brought an unexpected surprise. Since I was a little girl, I remember struggling with depression. As early as five or six years old, I was melancholic and saw the world as a glass half empty. I always felt like the underdog, struggled with insecurity, and doubted my abilities in school and life. Even when I succeeded, I would dismiss it as being lucky and always thought I would have to try harder next time or I would surely fail. Through my teens and early twenties, I was on antidepressants and depended on them to function. I thought I would take them for the rest of my life, but to my surprise, after my season of lament from my divorce, I have not experienced depression. I believe that I received complete healing from depressive moods through this practice. I truly believe that this healing occurred through obtaining a grateful heart that came from the daily renewed perspective that I gained through the process of lament. While I know life is not perfect, the process of lament has brought physical, mental, and spiritual healing that I never knew I could experience.

REFLECTION QUESTIONS

1. Are you dealing with feelings of loneliness and abandonment? How are you processing these feelings, for example, avoidance, busyness, isolation?
2. How do Psalms 42–43 help you think differently about lament?
3. How can we honestly express our emotions but also speak truth to our souls?

4. How can you reach out to your community during this time? How can your community be one that reaches out to those who are experiencing loneliness and abandonment?

INDIVIDUAL PRACTICE

Spend some time with the Lord expressing your honest emotions. Ask him to fill the loneliness that you are experiencing at this moment. Find a podcast or sermon on this subject and listen to it. Journal about what stood out to you as you listened. Ask the Lord to lead you into the next steps. Perhaps you need to text a friend, join a small group, or attend a service at church? Be open and willing to follow through.

CORPORATE PRACTICE

Cultivate a culture in your church or community that is not just focused on families or couples. Try to be mindful of individuals and to actively incorporate them. Do not see them as add-ons. Brainstorm about how you can encourage single, divorced, and widowed individuals to be part of the community, especially during the holiday season.

9

Lament and Sickness/Physical Pain

Suffering that comes from physical pain and sickness can be exhausting. Many people deal with life-threatening illnesses or physical pain that require surgery or extensive medical treatment. There are also those who suffer from chronic pain. A recent article on chronic pain found that 50.2 million adults in the United States (20.5 percent) reported pain on most days or every day. The study also reported that those who suffered from this type of pain experienced limitations in daily function, including work, social activities, and daily living. The most common pain-management strategies were physical therapy and massage.[1] While there are benefits to these management strategies on the physical level, there are often emotional and even spiritual burdens that accompany physical pain and sickness. Lament is not a magic bullet or remedy to the emotional and spiritual suffering associated with physical pain and sickness, but it does help provide an avenue to help us process these struggles.

Several psalms mention physical pain and suffering as a reason for lament, for example, Psalms 6; 38; 88; 102. In the New Testament, the apostle Paul laments the thorn in his side. The thorn has never been conclusively identified, but some commentators suggest that it could have been a physical ailment.

---

[1] R. Jason Yong, Peter M. Mullins, and Neil Bhattacharyya, "Prevalence of Chronic Pain Among Adults in the United States," *Pain* 163, no. 2 (2022): e328-e332.

We live in a fallen world, and illness and pain are unavoidable. Every year that I grow older, I feel my body becoming more susceptible to pain and illness. I find that even bruises and injuries take longer to heal. My body just does not bounce back or cooperate as it used to. But when pains or illnesses are acute, severe, life threatening, or debilitating due to their chronic nature, how should we respond? What can lament teach us? In this chapter, I want to highlight Psalm 88, which deals with physical pain that could possibly lead to death and mental struggles as well as social ostracism. This psalm is characterized as one of the bleakest psalms, if not the bleakest in the collection, because it does not end in hope. In fact, in the Hebrew the final word in this psalm is *darkness*. Even though the psalm does not exhibit explicit words of hope, it is still instructive when we are dealing with severe sickness and physical pain because it provides a realistic reflection of someone struggling with an ongoing situation.

PSALM 88

Lord, you are the God who saves me;
    day and night I cry out to you.
May my prayer come before you;
    turn your ear to my cry.
I am overwhelmed with troubles
    and my life draws near to death.
I am counted among those who go down to the pit;
    I am like one without strength.
I am set apart with the dead,
    like the slain who lie in the grave,
whom you remember no more,
    who are cut off from your care.
You have put me in the lowest pit,
    in the darkest depths.
Your wrath lies heavily on me;
    you have overwhelmed me with all your waves.
You have taken from me my closest friends
    and have made me repulsive to them.
I am confined and cannot escape;
    my eyes are dim with grief.

> I call to you, LORD, every day;
>   I spread out my hands to you.
> Do you show your wonders to the dead?
>   Do their spirits rise up and praise you?
> Is your love declared in the grave,
>   your faithfulness in Destruction?
> Are your wonders known in the place of darkness,
>   or your righteous deeds in the land of oblivion?
> But I cry to you for help, LORD;
>   in the morning my prayer comes before you.
> Why, LORD, do you reject me
>   and hide your face from me?
> From my youth I have suffered and been close to death;
>   I have borne your terrors and am in despair.
> Your wrath has swept over me;
>   your terrors have destroyed me.
> All day long they surround me like a flood;
>   they have completely engulfed me.
> You have taken from me friend and neighbor—
>   darkness is my closest friend.

Recall that the following five elements are characteristic of laments. As mentioned before, not all elements will be present in every lament, and they may not follow this order.

- address or invocation
- lamentation/petition/complaint
- motivations
- confession of trust/assurance of being heard
- vow of praise

Address or invocation. This poem opens with an address to Yahweh (Ps 88:1 [2]). However, unlike other psalms, the psalmist also calls God "the God of my salvation" (NIV, "the God who saves me"). This is important because even in a psalm that lacks explicit words of hope, the psalmist begins his prayer by acknowledging that God is the only who can save, and that is why the psalmist cries out to him. The psalmist knows that there is no other place to which he can turn for help, so he comes in prayer continually before God. In Psalms, the noun *yĕšû'â*, "salvation," and the verb *yāša'*, "to save," refer primarily to Yahweh. According to the *Theological Dictionary of the Old Testament*, "The subject is always God, except where God is contrasted to the vanity of human aid (Ps. 60:13 [11]; 108:13 [12]; cf. 146:3; Lam. 4:17) or the inadequacy of military might (Ps. 33:16f.; 44:4, 6 [3, 5])."[2] Though the psalmist properly addresses the only one who can bring true salvation, this does not mean that prayer alone is all we need when we are facing physical illness or pain. We should seek the necessary medical treatments and doctors to help treat these issues, but we must also acknowledge that God is the ultimate healer of our bodies, soul and spirit. For instance, King Hezekiah in Isaiah 38:9-20 laments his illness in prayer, and he also applies the remedy that is necessary for his recovery in Isaiah 38:21.

Notice that this is not a "one and done" prayer. Psalm 88:1 [2] says, "Day and night I cry out to you." The psalmist continually calls out to God because he desires his prayers to be heard. This prayer is not a formula or incantation. No, his cries stem from a heartfelt need to be heard and healed. In our struggle, we must remember that God is there, even when we feel weak or are tired of enduring the physical pain that plagues our body. We must press into God through our prayers and learn to remain in his presence in the midst of our pains. It is easy to give into numbness and apathy emotionally because we are physically spent, but turning to God in our weakness is where we will find our strength.

I am reminded of John 15:1-4, where Jesus tells us that God, our Father, is the master gardener who prunes or cuts off branches so that we can be more fruitful. When a master gardener prunes off branches, he sometimes must cut off branches that seem to be flourishing or even flowering to make the vine even more fruitful. The process seems counterintuitive and is not pleasant to endure. Cutting away is never easy because it is a process of loss. Physical mobility, appetite, sleep, and the ability to complete daily activities are only a few of the losses we can experience when

---

[2]John F.A. Sawyer, "ישע," *Theological Dictionary of the Old Testament*, ed. G. Johannes Botterweck and Helmer Ringgren, trans. John T. Willis et al. (Grand Rapids, MI: Eerdmans, 1974–2006).

dealing with illness and pain. But in this process, we must trust that God, our master gardener, knows what is best. In this context Jesus reminds us that we must remain in him and let his words remain in us (Jn 15:4, 7). Remaining is a constant process. It is a willingness to stay put and allow God to work. We must trust that he is the one who knows what will come down the road and will work it out as he sees best. We can trust that in even when we are undergoing pruning, God will use these difficulties in our lives so that we can be even more fruitful than we were before. This is not easy, especially when we have no idea what this will look like. It is hard to remain and hold fast to God when we are in pain, but this is what Jesus calls us to do and what the psalmist is doing as he calls out day and night.

Psalm 88:1 also demonstrates a willingness on the part of the psalmist to continue dialoguing with God. Even though his prayers are filled with honest complaints, doubts, and questions, his calling out to God and recognizing God's ability to bring salvation demonstrates that he has not given up. Instead of giving way to bitterness and anger, he turns to God in honesty, trusting that God is the one who can heal. When Hezekiah weeps bitterly because of his illness (2 Kings 20:3), God answers through the prophet Isaiah, saying, "I have heard your prayer and seen your tears; I will heal you" (2 Kings 20:5). This is not a promise that God will always heal, but it does show us that God hears our prayers and sees our tears.

Lamentation/petition/complaint. Here, the psalmist expresses feelings of pain and loneliness. While the language is general enough to encompass a variety of trials, the references to and images associated with death could point to one who is struggling with sickness. Several interpreters of the psalm have viewed this as a prayer for a very sick person who is near death.[3] Sickness indeed often causes us to reflect on death, though it is not the only situation that causes us to do so. "There is no difficulty in associating the psalm with serious and chronic (v 16) illness, but the metaphorical backdrop is wider than sickness and can encompass any severe

---

[3]Mitchell Dahood, *Psalms I: 1–50*, Anchor Bible (New Haven, CT: Yale University Press, 1995), 302; Marvin E. Tate, *Psalms 51–100*, Word Biblical Commentary (Nashville: Thomas Nelson, 1991), 401.

distress or life-threatening situation."[4] The psalmist here explicitly mentions death, Sheol, and the pit. Sheol is the place of the dead or the underworld, and "the pit" is another term used to refer to the place of the dead (see Ps 28:1; 30:4).

The psalmist also talks about the loss of his strength as he nears death. Notice how the content intensifies. The psalmist begins by describing his soul as full of trouble (Ps 88:3 [4]) and says that his life draws near to death (Ps 88:3 [4]). He then moves to being counted as one who actually goes down into the pit (Ps 88:4 [5]), and then sees himself as one who is slain and living in the grave, with God having no remembrance of him (Ps 88:5 [6]). As the psalm continues, he is completely cut off from God's hand or care (Ps 88:5 [6]). His situation gets progressively bleaker.

As is often the case when we are dealing with sickness and pain, our thoughts tend to spiral downward. In Psalm 88:3-4 [4-5] the psalmist uses first-person forms, *I* and *my*, to describe his state. His focus is on himself and his painful situation. While we do not exactly know what the psalmist was dealing with, we know that he is not dead yet. However, he feels as if he were just one step away from the grave and from being cut off from God. As he is processing his pain, his thoughts reflect a progression to what he feels is the inevitable outcome. Sometimes when we are dealing with terminal illness or severe physical pain, thoughts of death loom large in our minds. It is okay to express these fears in prayer to the Lord. We do not have to shy away from these thoughts before God. He is aware of our frailty and weaknesses.

The psalmist then transitions to address God. His lament moves into complaint. Specifically, he accuses God of putting him into the lowest pit and into dark places and deep darkness (Ps 88:6 [7]) and bemoans how God's wrath has been laid on him and how breaking waves have overwhelmed him (Ps 88:7 [8]). God has even removed his closest friends and made him an abomination or repulsive to them. He feels shut in and unable to escape (Ps 88:8 [9]). The psalmist does not hold back. He believes that God has brought about this struggle and has trapped him.

---

[4]Tate, *Psalms 51–100*, 401.

Lament and Sickness/Physical Pain

Such language, which also occurs in Lamentations 2:1-9 and Job 16:7-14, frames God as the enemy. The psalmist also returns to this language in Psalm 88:15-18 [16-19]. These verses seem to be almost the opposite from what we find in Psalm 88:1-2 [2-3], where the psalmist calls God the God of his salvation. Why is this type of language in this psalm? Is it okay to say these things to God?

Such language reflects what many feel when they are facing severe trials, whether terminal illness, terminal illness of a loved one, excruciating pain associated with sickness, or even acute chronic pain. When there is a disconnect with what we know to be true about God and what we are experiencing, we may have similar thoughts and feel similar emotions. However, many of us have been taught that this is wrong. We have been told that we should not speak to God this way or even think these things. But if you have ever experienced debilitating illness, chronic pain, or other physical agony, chances are these thoughts have crossed your mind. Instead of suppressing these thoughts and feelings, we need to learn, like the psalmist, to bring them before God. God can handle our doubts and complaints. In fact, sharing them with him builds intimacy. This is better than the alternative of letting bitterness stew in our hearts.

I was just speaking with someone who shared about a mutual friend who went through deep trauma from an unfaithful and abusive spouse who left him. He had been left alone and abandoned in the hospital for several months to recover from the physical abuse he experienced. He had lost all hope for living but had been able to slowly recover from the physical injuries. Although this had all happened several years ago, he never honestly dealt with the questions he had in God's presence. Instead, he kept everything bottled up inside. Even his own sister was unaware of the abuse in his marriage. He felt he could not speak openly about it with anyone because it would not have been right to do so. Now he questions God's existence, and over the last several years he has distanced himself from the church community. Instead of honestly wrestling with his pain and asking God why he would allow this to happen, he allowed this unresolved pain to result in alienation between himself and God as well as his church community. He thought he was doing the spiritual thing by keeping difficulties to himself and did not allow himself to honestly express the rawness of his pain, doubts, and questions before God. Unfortunately, this only led to a greater chasm between him and God.

William Harris summarizes how this type of expression by the psalmist displays a bold or robust faith. Instead of suppressing or denying the emotions that resulted from his near-death experience, expressing them before God is actually exhibiting a faith that is willing to wrestle with the incongruities between life and what we believe about God. This is a step toward God. Harris writes, "Voicing one's anger with respect to suffering is not only spiritually healthy, but necessary if spiritual health and intimacy with God is to be restored."[5]

Psalm 88 expresses similar feelings of anger in the midst of suffering. The psalmist feels like God has his wrath on him and has overwhelmed him. Psalm 88:9 [10] describes his state of grief. His eyes are languishing because of sorrow, but he continues to call out to God. In his complaint and grief, he does not give up on God; instead, he spreads out his hands to God in a posture of waiting (Ps 88:9 [10]). This is instructive for us when we are wading through difficult waters. If you are dealing with doubts and anger, bring them to God. Do not stop calling out to him in your pain. Do not shut down lines of communication. Come before him and call to him.

Motivations. The following verses in Psalm 88 provide the motivations for God to act and answer. The psalmist presents a series of rhetorical questions (Ps 88:10-12 [11-13]) as well as an affirmation that he is continually praying and crying out to the Lord (Ps 88:13 [14]). Notice how the psalmist appeals to God's lovingkindness, faithfulness, wonders, and righteous deeds in his questions. As we observed previously, in lament psalms the motivation for God to act is often closely associated with his character. In this psalm is it associated with his character and actions as a God of salvation. Again, the Hebrew words for lovingkindness (*ḥesed*) and faithfulness (*ʾĕmûnâ*) point to God's self-revelation in Exodus 34:6. The term *faithfulness*, when applied to God (Deut 32:4; Ps 33:4), describes his total

---

[5] William L. Harris III, "Psalm 88: A Validation to Vent," *Criswell Theological Journal* 55 (2020): 45.

dependability, and *lovingkindness* refers to God's love, mercy, and loyalty, especially displayed in the context of his covenant relationship with his people.

The Hebrew word for "wonders," *peleʾ*, in Psalm 88:12 [13] is used in association with God's powerful acts of deliverance in Exodus (Ex 15:11) as well as saving acts in the future (Is 25:1). Additionally, the word for righteous deeds (*ṣədāqâ*) in Psalm 88:12 [13] often speaks of God's righteousness and justice in association with salvation (Is 1:27; 46:13). By appealing to these specific attributes and works of God, the psalmist is appealing for God to act in consistency with his nature. Speaking of these attributes of God in the context of the grave, underworld, or land of oblivion highlights the importance of the idea of remembrance. How can God's character and deeds be declared if the psalmist goes to the grave? This could cause God's glory to be forgotten among the living. But the psalmist is quick to affirm that he does not want this to happen. In Psalm 88:13 [14], he begins with "But I." He is emphasizing that he will continue to cry and pray as long as he has breath so that God can demonstrate his love and power, which will result in the psalmist's praise.

Lamentation/petition/complaint. As noted earlier, this psalm does not have the elements of confession of trust/assurance of being heard or a vow of praise. Instead, it circles back to lamentation/petition/complaint. In the last section, the poet repeats the same themes of closeness to death (Ps 88:3-6 [4-7]), engulfing waters (Ps 88:7 [8]), and alienation (Ps 88:8 [9]). By circling back to these laments and complaints, the psalm is mirroring our emotions when we are dealing with illness or acute or chronic physical pain. It is never a straight upward trajectory. Rather, our emotions sometimes get the best us, and we have to reprocess our feelings and circumstances. While this psalm does not end on a hopeful note, this does not mean the psalmist has lost all hope. It provides a better reflection of real-life situations when we feel close to death. Instead of experiencing healing or resolution, the psalm shows the psalmist waiting on God in the darkness. It is significant that the last word of the psalm is "darkness" (*ḥōšek*). Like the psalmist, sometimes our resolution is still to come.

We are still in the mist of darkness. Our part is to wait on the Lord as we express our honest feelings before him.

Pain and illness can plague us on many levels and in different ways. For this reason, I decided to include two stories in this section. The first story is a journey through pain experienced by a close friend during years of physical suffering. The second is a story of a mother lamenting over her child's struggle with cancer. Sometimes we may not be the ones going through the pain, but we still practice lament because our loved ones' suffering hurts us deeply as well.

Susanne's Story

I was silently dying, battling an eating disorder, anorexia nervosa, for the past thirty-plus years, unknowingly living as a survivor of childhood trauma, including sexual abuse. From his mercy, God, through Jesus Christ, became my true Heavenly Father, who loved me deeply. This truth was and still is my reality, helping me through all the trials and hardships throughout my life. However, in my mid-forties, I woke up one early November morning, so exhausted and weak I could not get out of bed without the help of my husband. I was immediately hospitalized, and the Lord took me on my journey of true brokenness. The day before, I had been heading toward the pinnacle of my career, a position only about 1 percent in my field could achieve. In the eyes of the world, I had everything: marriage, family, wealth, academic success, health, status. In an instant, my health was gone, and so was my career.

For the next three years, my life consisted of almost-daily doctor's appointments, blood tests, various x-rays, CT scans, MRIs, painful procedures, surgeries, and frequent trips to the emergency room. I was unaware that I was in imminent danger of losing my life. The complex consequences of a yearslong eating disorder had ravaged my body physically, exhausted my emotional capacity, and left me in the pains of depression. I required life-sustaining medical support, including several bouts of long-term intravenous nutrition, feeding tubes, and even a major surgery to reconstruct my colon. A complication after a procedure caused me to be treated in the ICU for an emergency surgery and medical support to

Lament and Sickness/Physical Pain

prevent septic shock. I remembered opening my eyes and seeing about twelve IV pumps, pouring medications and IV fluids into my veins to keep me alive. How had my life come to this?

Recovery was slow and painful. Many days I would open my eyes in the morning, wishing it was evening so I could go back to sleep, then sighing in relief in the evenings when I could return to the only time I had temporary relief in my physical and emotional pain: sleep. Sleep was induced and was successful only with high doses of a cocktail of various medications. When it was unsuccessful, I suffered from insomnia and pain, a terrible combination that can be summed up as a pit of lonely despair. It took control over my body and mind. However, in those dark days, in a pit that sometimes felt bottomless, I knew God, my loving Heavenly Father, who knew me before I was born, was sitting with me in the pit. My hope was not in the here and now but in Christ and knowing that one day, this short life on this side of heaven will be done, and I will have a new healthy and perfect body in heaven. My hope is in knowing that one day, he will invite me into heaven, wiping away my tears of sorrow, where there will be no more pain or sadness. This hope in Jesus gave me the strength to press on every day.

As the days, weeks, months, and years passed, the acute pain transitioned into invisible, chronic, long-term pain that even I was tired of hearing myself talk about. Who else could I unload this burden on, except Jesus? Sometimes I could only express myself in tears of despair and/or through the silence of depression. I had to take it one day at a time and sometimes one moment at a time.

It has now been almost nine years since that first day in the hospital. I can see several scars from past surgeries and procedures. I am painfully aware of an outward scar from the surgery to reconstruct my colon, and even worse, the emotional scar that left my colon permanently altered, a disability invisible to others. I have been asked how I was able to hold onto my faith and whether I ever blame or get mad at God. The answer is that my faith in Christ is a gift freely given to me at the cost of his life, and I never blamed or became angry at God. Why? Such a simple answer, yet so profound: because I know that my Heavenly Father deeply loves me.

This did not take away the pain and suffering that I endured, but I hung on to the hope that he always will be faithful, and his mercies are new every morning.

Anvita's story

As I sat on my rocking chair with my eyes closed and tears flooding down my face, I heard the Holy Spirit say, "Eyes on Jesus." He gave me an image of a fierce storm with thunder, lightning, and waves crashing all around me as I walked on water and saw a figure in the distance, who was Jesus. He was telling me that it was possible to walk on water in the middle of my storm as long as I kept my eyes on him.

A week prior to this, my husband and our two sons had gone to an apple orchard. While we were there, our son Isaiah started complaining of back pain. It was very unusual for him to complain. So, the next day we took him to the doctor's office. They did some tests, and we were sent to a specialist that same day. Isaiah, who had just turned three years old, was diagnosed with leukemia. We chose to get admitted to the same hospital where I was planning on delivering our third son. I had been on bed rest with him and expected his arrival at any time. That evening as I sat in the hospital room watching Isaiah sleep, I was paralyzed with fear. Then God gave me a verse from the book of Isaiah. "So do not fear, for I am with you; do not be dismayed, for I am your God. I will strengthen you and help you; I will uphold you with my righteous right hand" (Is 41:10). When I read "for I am your God," in just a few seconds he reminded me of the times that he had been faithful to me, provided for me, strengthened me, comforted me, protected me, never left me. I went from being completely gripped with fear to having his peace that surpasses all understanding wash over me.

We were admitted to the hospital for a week, where my son went through intense chemotherapy. The hardest thing I have done in life is to watch my child suffer. It was gut-wrenching to watch my son go through all the procedures, pain, and side effects of the medications. When we were discharged home, I was getting ready for our new normal for the next four years. I sat in that rocking chair and started thinking about the reality of things: I could give birth at any moment; we did not have family in town to help us; I had just been told I could not work for a year; we did not have a financial plan to pay our bills. As the tears started flooding while I sat on that rocking chair, the Holy Spirit reminded me to keep my eyes on Jesus.

I did just that. But in the middle of the chaos, the uncertainty, I was also brutally honest with God about my fears, my needs, and my desires. Every day throughout the day and night I would make my needs known to him. I had never been closer to Jesus more than in that season. I remember one time I was reading a book to my kids, and I could not stay awake. I kept dozing off, and every time I woke up, I said, *"Jesus."* My soul cried out to him day and night. Life did not get easier; in fact, we had more new health changes in our family that year. Every day was mentally, physically, emotionally exhausting. But I choose to share all my daily struggles and needs with him. It is the only reason I did not lose my sanity in those years. I learned that my God cares for all my needs, no matter how big or small. He is always available and true to all his promises.

REFLECTION QUESTIONS

1. How has your illness/pain or the illness/pain of a loved one affected you emotionally?
2. How can the practice of lament help you to reflect honestly on your emotions during this time?
3. How does the fact that Psalm 88 ends with waiting help you as you wait on God through this time?
4. How can the practice of lament help us to remember that it is a process and we can take things moment by moment?

INDIVIDUAL PRACTICE

If you or a loved one is experiencing pain, spend some moments journaling or praying your feelings, fears, and even anger toward God. Allow yourself the freedom to be brutally honest and let your tears flow if necessary. Allow yourself the freedom to be weak before God. Spend some time reading a passage from Scripture that speaks of God's care and faithfulness. If you can't think of one, perhaps you can meditate on Isaiah 41:10: "So do not fear, for I am with you; do not be dismayed, for I am your God. I will strengthen you and help you; I will uphold you with my righteous right hand." Let those words sink in. Sit in silence and reread the words. Pray your honest thoughts before the Lord as you read these words, even if you have trouble believing them. Let him know and ask for his strength. Wait on God to give you the next steps, no matter how small. Maybe it is just closing your eyes and sleeping, or it may be taking a few steps to the window to look outside. Allow yourself the freedom to wait on the Lord for his help during this time.

CORPORATE PRACTICE

If you know of an individual in your community, church, or small group who is in the hospital or home hospice, see whether you can help the family members who are on caretaking duty. Perhaps members in the church can take a shift to visit the individual to talk, pray, or sit in silence with them. This would give the caretaker some reprieve and allow time for members in the church to come alongside the ill or dying person.

10

Lament and Death/Loss

Mourning over the death of a loved one or loss is not a foreign concept to the Bible. Death and loss are difficulties that plague us all. Even Jesus weeps over the death of Lazarus.

The previous chapters have discussed lament in situations that are not necessarily final, meaning there is still room for change or improvement. However, when a death has occurred, there is a sense of finality that is different. This is why some make a distinction between laments and funeral dirges. Dirges can be considered a subcategory of communal laments, though they exhibit some differences from what is usually characteristic of communal laments. Generally communal laments ask for a reversal of the current state or the prevention of destruction. Conversely, dirges commonly express grief for losses that have already occurred (Ps 79:2-3; Lam 5:7). They usually call the community to mourn, or they announce a funeral. Some dirges also address citywide or national disasters, such as those found in ancient Near Eastern city laments (discussed in chapter three).

The distinction between laments and dirges is not as clear cut as we might like. The Hebrew term that coordinates with the English word *lament* as we usually think of lament is *qînâ* (*qînôt* in the plural). The English title for the book of Lamentations comes from this term, though, oddly, the word *qînôt*, "lamentations," is not found in Lamentations.

It was probably adopted as the title because it reflects the character of the book. The singular form *qînâ*, "lament," technically refers to a biblical funeral dirge or a eulogy. It is used in contexts such as 2 Samuel 1:17, where David writes a *qînâ* for Saul and Jonathan, or in 2 Samuel 3:33, where he laments over Abner. Similarly, this term can also be used to grieve the destruction of a city, such as Tyre in Ezekiel 27:32.

A *qînâ* can refer to a song or poem performed at a funeral. It was custom in the Jewish culture to hire lamenters or professional grievers for a funeral. The Mishnah, the oldest authoritative, postbiblical collection of Jewish oral laws, describes how to perform a *qînâ*. It states, "A woman recites and another repeats after her. The refrain may also mark an alternation between solo and chorus" (Mishnah Moʻed Qaṭan 3:9). In the ancient Near East, funerals were also characterized by weeping, mourning, tearing one's garment, wearing sackcloth, and wailing in ashes for several days (see Gen 50:10). Prominent Old Testament scholar Adele Berlin notes, "Although no actual *qinah* from the biblical period survives (the *qinot* we have in narrative and prophetic discourse are literary creations that presumably imitate actual dirges), we may conclude from numerous references to it that the qinah was a well-established genre of poetry used for the mourning of individuals."[1] For example, Jeremiah 31:15 describes Rachel weeping for her children and refusing to be comforted, and this verse is quoted in Matthew 2:18.

The biblical passage we will examine here is different from the previous chapters in that it is not a psalm. Instead, we will focus on Lamentations 1. While this chapter of Lamentations does have some of the elements common to biblical laments, it is also different because it contains elements of a dirge, that is, mourning loss and death. Some scholars, such as F. W. Dobbs-Allsopp, also compare Lamentations 1 to ancient Near Eastern city laments.[2] Before examining the elements of lament and dirge found in Lamentations 1, I will provide some general information on the

---

[1] Adele Berlin, *Lamentations: A Commentary*, Old Testament Library (Louisville, KY: Westminster John Knox, 2002), 23.
[2] See F. W. Dobbs-Allsopp, *Weep, O Daughter of Zion: A Study of the City-Lament Genre in the Hebrew Bible* (Rome: Gregorian & Biblical Press, 1993).

book of Lamentations as well as the structure of this first chapter to give a better understanding of its content and context.

INTRODUCTION TO THE BOOK OF LAMENTATIONS

Lamentations is a carefully structured work that provides a description of the devastation and despair experienced by those who witnessed the atrocities surrounding the destruction of Jerusalem by the Babylonians in 586/587 BC. The destruction was precipitated by a severe famine and siege that sent the surviving inhabitants off into exile. More specifics on the events that took place can be found in 2 Kings 25:1-21 and Jeremiah 52. However, if you read the book of Lamentations carefully, you will see that it does not mention any specific historical data. For example, the Babylonians are not named, the king's name is not given, and the dates are not provided. There are only descriptions about hunger, captivity, death, fire, and destruction. Because of this lack of historical information, the dating for this book falls broadly between 586 and 425 BC. While the book has been historically associated with the prophet Jeremiah, scholars are not in full agreement about this connection due to the lack of evidence as well as the inconsistency between the character of this book and Jeremiah's other works.[3]

Additionally, in the Hebrew Bible, Lamentations is not found after the book of Jeremiah. Instead, it is part of a special collection called the *Megillot* or Festival Scrolls. There are five books in this collection (also Song of Songs, Ruth, Ecclesiastes, Esther), and each of them is read during a specific Jewish holiday or festival. Lamentations is recited as part of a liturgical tradition on various feast days in the Jewish calendar. More specifically, it is solemnly read on the ninth of Ab, which commemorates the destruction of the temple by the Babylonians in 586 BC as well as by the Romans in AD 70. In Christian history, Lamentations has been read during the services of Tenebrae, which is associated with the evenings of Wednesday, Thursday, and Friday of Holy Week.

The book is composed of five poems that can be read individually or collectively. It is the Old Testament book with the most poetic devices

---

[3]See Claus Westermann, *Lamentations: Issues and Interpretation* (Minneapolis: Fortress, 1994), xiii-xvii.

employed. Perhaps the most obvious device for Jewish readers is the acrostic structure, which provides a frame for the book. The first four chapters or poems are arranged in a formally defined acrostic pattern. Each poetic section or strophe begins with a letter that is alphabetically ordered according to the Hebrew alphabet. However, the acrostic feature is not uniform throughout the book. Lamentations 1 and Lamentations 2 have three lines in each of their twenty-two strophes/twenty-two verses, which corresponds to the twenty-two letters of the Hebrew alphabet. Lamentations 3 is an intensified acrostic. Instead of having only the first line of the strophe beginning with a Hebrew letter in alphabetic order, all three lines in each of the twenty-two strophes (66 verses) begin with the same Hebrew letter in alphabetic order. Lamentations 4 reverts back to only the first line in the strophe beginning with the Hebrew letter in alphabetic order. However, in Lamentations 4, instead of having three lines for each of its twenty-two strophes, there are only two lines per strophe (22 verses). Lamentations 5 only has twenty-two lines (22 verses) and no acrostic.

Table 10.1. Structure of Lamentations

Chapter 1	Chapter 2	Chapter 3	Chapter 4	Chapter 5
22 strophes (verses)	22 strophes (verses)	22 strophes (verses)	22 strophes (verses)	22 strophes (verses)
Three lines per strophe	Three lines per strophe	Three lines per strophe	Two lines per strophe	One line per strophe
One letter per strophe	One letter per strophe	One letter per strophe	One letter per strophe	No alphabetic sequence
66 lines	66 lines	66 lines	44 lines	22 lines
a ___ ___	a ___ ___	a a a	a ___	___

Another prominent poetic feature in this book is the change in voice. In Lamentations 1, there are two voices. The first half of the book is mainly the narrator, who speaks in third person, describing Lady Jerusalem's situation. Lady Jerusalem speaks in the remaining half of the book using first-person forms. The division occurs in the middle of the poem, which corresponds to the midpoint of the Hebrew alphabet. This division reinforces the structural frame.

Imagery, personification, and metaphors are also rich in the book. In Lamentations 1, the city of Jerusalem is personified as a grieving woman. The author does this to shape how the audience experiences the information described. This aspect personalizes the experience of Jerusalem as it depicts her as a suffering woman who sits alone, even though in reality it is describing the experience of the city collectively. By attributing human characteristics to the nonhuman entity of a city, the author helps the audience to relate more fully to the suffering and loss described. The images in this first chapter all highlight the dire state of the city and her grief and loss. Let us examine this poem more closely to understand how lament can help us during times of death and loss.

LAMENTATIONS 1

> How deserted lies the city,
>   once so full of people!
> How like a widow is she,
>   who once was great among the nations!
> She who was queen among the provinces
>   has now become a slave.
> Bitterly she weeps at night,
>   tears are on her cheeks.
> Among all her lovers
>   there is no one to comfort her.
> All her friends have betrayed her;
>   they have become her enemies.
> After affliction and harsh labor,
>   Judah has gone into exile.
> She dwells among the nations;
>   she finds no resting place.
> All who pursue her have overtaken her
>   in the midst of her distress.
> The roads to Zion mourn,
>   for no one comes to her appointed festivals.

All her gateways are desolate,
    her priests groan,
her young women grieve,
    and she is in bitter anguish.
Her foes have become her masters;
    her enemies are at ease.
The Lord has brought her grief
    because of her many sins.
Her children have gone into exile,
    captive before the foe.
All the splendor has departed
    from Daughter Zion.
Her princes are like deer
    that find no pasture;
in weakness they have fled
    before the pursuer.
In the days of her affliction and wandering
    Jerusalem remembers all the treasures
    that were hers in days of old.
When her people fell into enemy hands,
    there was no one to help her.
Her enemies looked at her
    and laughed at her destruction.
Jerusalem has sinned greatly
    and so has become unclean.
All who honored her despise her,
    for they have all seen her naked;
she herself groans
    and turns away.
Her filthiness clung to her skirts;
    she did not consider her future.
Her fall was astounding;
    there was none to comfort her.
"Look, Lord, on my affliction,
    for the enemy has triumphed."

The enemy laid hands
    on all her treasures;
she saw pagan nations
    enter her sanctuary—
those you had forbidden
    to enter your assembly.
All her people groan
    as they search for bread;
they barter their treasures for food
    to keep themselves alive.
"Look, LORD, and consider,
    for I am despised."
"Is it nothing to you, all you who pass by?
    Look around and see.
Is any suffering like my suffering
    that was inflicted on me,
that the LORD brought on me
    in the day of his fierce anger?
"From on high he sent fire,
    sent it down into my bones.
He spread a net for my feet
    and turned me back.
He made me desolate,
    faint all the day long.
"My sins have been bound into a yoke;
    by his hands they were woven together.
They have been hung on my neck,
    and the Lord has sapped my strength.
He has given me into the hands
    of those I cannot withstand.
"The Lord has rejected
    all the warriors in my midst;
he has summoned an army against me
    to crush my young men.
In his winepress the Lord has trampled
    Virgin Daughter Judah.

"This is why I weep
    and my eyes overflow with tears.
No one is near to comfort me,
    no one to restore my spirit.
My children are destitute
    because the enemy has prevailed."
Zion stretches out her hands,
    but there is no one to comfort her.
The Lord has decreed for Jacob
    that his neighbors become his foes;
Jerusalem has become
    an unclean thing among them.
"The Lord is righteous,
    yet I rebelled against his command.
Listen, all you peoples;
    look on my suffering.
My young men and young women
    have gone into exile.
"I called to my allies
    but they betrayed me.
My priests and my elders
    perished in the city
while they searched for food
    to keep themselves alive.
"See, Lord, how distressed I am!
    I am in torment within,
and in my heart I am disturbed,
    for I have been most rebellious.
Outside, the sword bereaves;
    inside, there is only death.
"People have heard my groaning,
    but there is no one to comfort me.
All my enemies have heard of my distress;
    they rejoice at what you have done.
May you bring the day you have announced
    so they may become like me.

> "Let all their wickedness come before you;
>   deal with them
>   as you have dealt with me
>   because of all my sins.
>   My groans are many
>   and my heart is faint."

Recall that the following five elements are characteristic of laments. As mentioned before, not all elements will be present in every lament, and they may not follow this order.

- address or invocation
- lamentation/petition/complaint
- motivations
- confession of trust/assurance of being heard
- vow of praise

As mentioned earlier, this chapter contains elements characteristic of biblical laments as well as elements characteristic of dirges. The lament elements are seen most clearly in the speeches of Lady Jerusalem, while the dirge elements are featured in the narrator's descriptions. Lamentations 1 can be divided into two parts. The main speaker in the first half of the poem is the narrator (Lam 1:11), but Lady Jerusalem interjects in Lamentations 1:9. She then becomes the main speaker in the second half of the poem (Lam 1:12-22), and the narrator interjects in her speech in Lamentations 1:15c, 17. There are two distinct speeches by Lady Jerusalem, addressed to observers who pass by, first in Lamentations 1:12-16 and second in Lamentations 1:18-19. She also cries out to God three times (Lam 1:9, 11, 20-22).

The first half of the poem opens with a description by the narrator of Lady Jerusalem's situation. The narrator speaks as a third-party observer describing what he sees and highlights several facets of her grief and loss. First, Lady Jerusalem is described as all alone and grieving the loss of her loved ones. She was once full of people, but now she has become like a widow (Lam 1:1). Her situation gets worse; she is not only grieving the loss of loved ones, but she is also experiencing serious loss. She has lost her status as a princess and her greatness among the nations. In fact, she who was once served by others must now serve as a slave to others, not by choice but through forced labor (Lam 1:1).

The chapter opens with the Hebrew interjection *ʾêkâ* ("Alas! How! Oh! Ah!"), which is also the Hebrew title of the book. This exclamation is often associated with funeral dirges (Jer 48:17; Ezek 26:17). By opening the chapter with this word, the narrator prepares the audience to encounter the image of a widow. These first few verses depict emptiness and loss. Jerusalem is a widow who sits alone and has lost her husband as well as her children. Her former state of fullness and greatness is now a memory. The narrator provides vivid descriptions associated with mourning and grief. Additionally, Lady Jerusalem has no comforter. Her loved ones and friends have rejected her and even have become her enemies (Lam 1:2). She is left weeping all alone. The lack of a comforter or helper is repeated six times in the poem (see Lam 1:2, 7, 9, 16-17, 21).

The images then shift in Lamentations 1:3-5 to highlight another aspect of her plight. Exile and homelessness are presented through the image of a refugee who has been overtaken by her captors (Lam 1:3). Barren roads and gates (Lam 1:4), and the subjugation of her people, including women and children before their enemies (Lam 1:5), emphasize this plight. Images of displacement, loss, and regret as well as shame fill these verses. There is no more celebration with the loss of the temple (Lam 1:4); only desolation and shame remain. Judah and Jerusalem recognize that their failure to keep the covenant promises has resulted in this affliction (Lam 1:8). The Lord warned them in Deuteronomy 28:15-68 about the consequences and curses associated with the breaking of the covenant. He sent countless prophets to warn them, but they continued in their apostasy and rejection of the Lord.

Lamentations 1:8-10 describes the sad reversal of Lady Jerusalem. Her splendor has departed, her enemies have triumphed, and she is left with affliction, shame, and wandering. This reversal theme further highlights the city's current plight. She was not just any city; she was a city set apart. Now she is destroyed, and her inhabitants have gone into exile. This

Lament and Death/Loss

major change in status is a stark contrast to her former state. While Jerusalem's culpability and sin are acknowledged, the focus of this chapter is not on her sin but on her immense suffering. The imagery emphasizes her loss, pain, and lack of a comforter. As the poem begins, the narration in this first half sets the context for a dirge; however, what we encounter in Lady Jerusalem's prayer (in the second half) displays the elements found in individual lament psalms.

Address or invocation. As mentioned earlier, the narrator is the main voice in the first half of the chapter, but Lady Jerusalem interjects in Lamentations 1:9. Instead of staying silent or turning to the narrator, she cries out to God. Notice that her cry comes right after the narrator restates that there is no one to comfort her. In her recognition that there is no physical comforter, she turns to the Lord. Like in most individual laments, she begins her prayer with a cry to God. Her immediate request is for God to take notice of her dejected state and the triumph of her enemy. More specifically, she uses the imperative form of the verb "to see," *rā'āh*, translated as "Look." Her suffering and grief are too much, and her only recourse is to turn to the only one who can help her. She knows that there is nowhere else to go. Even in situations of profound loss and grief, only Yahweh truly understands and can comfort us.

Even more noteworthy is that Jerusalem's situation is tainted with personal sin and disobedience. Even though this is the case, she still turns to God because he is the only true comforter and healer. The narrator then continues to describe the desolate state of the nation in Lamentations 1:10-11, and then Lady Jerusalem speaks again. This time there is a transition, and Lady Jerusalem becomes the main speaker until the end of the poem. Each time she addresses the Lord throughout the book, she begins with same verb. By asking God to look, she is actually asking God to act. In Exodus 3:7-8, the Lord says, "I have indeed seen the misery of my people in Egypt. I have heard them crying out because of their slave drivers, and I am concerned about their suffering. So I have come down to rescue them." The words "indeed seen" are a double usage of the same verb *rā'āh*. Additionally, the words for misery and suffering used in the Exodus passage are the same words used to describe Lady Jerusalem's misery in Lamentations 1:7 and suffering in Lamentations 1:12, 18. Because God saw and heard in Exodus and acted out of compassion, Lady Jerusalem is asking for God to do it again in her own situation of misery and suffering.

Lamentation/petition/complaint. After turning to Yahweh again, Lady Jerusalem then turns to those who pass by (Lam 1:12) and asks them to compare her suffering. She is lamenting what the Lord has brought on her because of his fierce anger (Lam 1:12). God is depicted as one who has inflicted pain on her (Lam 1:12), but she acknowledges that this is also a consequence of her sin and rebellion (Lam 1:14, 18-19). Again, the focus is not on her sin here but on her suffering. She weeps over the loss of her young men (Lam 1:15) and the desolation her children face because the enemy has prevailed (Lam 1:16). However, she recognizes that her enemies have gained the upper hand because God has allowed it to be so (Lam 1:15).

In Lamentations 1:15c, 17 the narrator interjects into Lady Jerusalem's speech and restates that she has suffered loss, has no comforter, and God has even decreed Israel's enemies to be against his own people (Lam 1:17). While Lady Jerusalem acknowledges her sin, she still calls out for the people to look on her suffering, especially because she has lost so many young men and women who have gone into exile (Lam 1:18). Affirming what the narrator has said, she laments that her allies have betrayed her (Lam 1:19). With nowhere to go, she turns to God again (Lam 1:20). Again, she begins with the verb *rāʾāh*, "to see." She is desperately imploring God to see how distressed she is. The torment in her heart is overwhelming, and all she witnesses is death (Lam 1:20). The loss is overwhelming, and she has no one to comfort her (Lam 1:21). Her enemies are rejoicing over her distress and destruction.

While Lady Jerusalem's situation involves sin, this does not lessen her pain. That the poem's focus is on the suffering and not the sin does not make light of or skirt the issue of sin. There may be times when we are facing difficulties and loss that we start to question whether God is repaying us for sins that we have committed or wonder whether we are dealing with consequences of our decisions. Regardless of whether this is actually the case, this is not where our thoughts should remain. God has not abandoned us in our pain due to our own sin and bad decisions. Other times our situations are merely the result of living in a fallen world. All suffering is painful, and Lamentations acknowledges that. Pain should not be marginalized, regardless of its cause. Scripture acknowledges our pain in loss and death and does not make light of suffering.

A variety of emotions occur when we grieve. They can range from numbness to depression to anger. We may feel like there is no comforter, but God is the true comforter. Even if we are turning to others to see our pain, we must also turn to the Lord. Even if we feel shame because it has been a while since we have turned to him, like Lady Jerusalem, we ought to come and cry out to God. We are not to hide or run away but rather process the emotions in God's presence. Notice how Lady Jerusalem recounts all the things that have happened to her and her people. She repeats many of the themes the narrator already described in the first half of the chapter. Similarly, we should make room to process and even recount things that have transpired with their accompanying emotions. Has it been a hard year? Has it been a hard season? Have you lost someone close? Bring these thoughts and feelings before the Lord. Have you felt emotionally depleted and rejected? Bring that before God. Have you lost all motivation to move forward? Has this loss left you feeling alone and lifeless? Tell it God, or simply sit in his presence in silence. He understands and he sees. Nothing, not sin, not even death, can separate us from his love.

Motivations. The motivation element in biblical lament usually provides reasons for God to act or move toward action. In the last two verses (Lam 1:21-22), Lady Jerusalem appeals to God's justice to judge and deal with her enemies. Her enemies have heard of her distress, and instead of showing compassion, they rejoice. She asks God to bring retributive justice so that they will become like her (Lam 1:21). Her desire appeals to verses such as Proverbs 17:5, "Whoever gloats over disaster will not go unpunished." In the closing verse, she asks that their evil would come before God and that God would deal in justice with them, just as he has dealt with her transgressions. Like the psalms of imprecation, Lady Jerusalem is asking for justice. This is not just revenge but freedom from the evil that she has been subjugated to. While not all situations of death and loss require justice, there times when the death of a loved one is the result of evil. At those moments, we can leave justice in the hands of God.

As noted above, the literary form of this poem is different from those found in Psalms. The first half is the narrator providing a third-party witness to Lady Jerusalem's calamity, painting a dire picture of loss and destruction. In the speeches of Lady Jerusalem are only the first three elements of lament: address or invocation, lamentation/petition/complaint, and motivations. Like in Psalm 88, the last two elements of confession of trust/assurance of being heard and a vow of praise are absent. Perhaps because Lamentations 1 is dealing primarily with death, loss, and grief, it does not necessarily transition easily to joy.

Processing illness and physical pain can take a long time; however, because death is final, it is different in that a new normal must be realized through mourning. Grief can linger for years. Holidays and anniversaries can trigger feelings all over again. There will be days the loss seems more unbearable. When that happens, do not rush the process. Remember that you do not have to make leaps and bounds. Just take one step forward. Maybe it is writing a few sentences in your journal about how you are thankful for the person you lost. Maybe it is sitting in God's presence and just letting your tears roll down. Maybe it is meeting with a friend to pray together. Sometimes it is just getting up and brushing your teeth and combing your hair. Your emotional health is like your physical health. Small steps in the right direction are required to bring you to a place where you feel healthy again.

Grief resulting from the death of a loved one is probably one of the most universal and difficult experiences we have in life. The emptiness we feel after a loss will not just go away if we suppress it or busy ourselves. We must grieve the loss and accept comfort from others as well as the Lord. Learning to adjust to a world now lacking someone we loved requires support from those around us. Studies have shown that social connection is very important when someone loses a loved one. This does not mean that we must start going to parties or large gatherings; instead, it encourages us to find a small group of friends who will support us through this time. In other words, we need people who are willing to witness our pain and provide comfort. This is exactly what the repeated refrain about Lady Jerusalem lacking a comforter emphasizes. She is looking for someone to witness her pain and comfort her. She turns to God as well as others for this comfort.

This aspect of witnessing is also important to remember when we have friends who are grieving. Instead of avoiding them because of discomfort or feeling like we do not know what to do or say, we can learn to simply be present during this time. Maybe this means that we sit with them in silence over tea or coffee. Maybe this means that we write them a card letting them know that we care for and hurt with them. Maybe this means we allow them to cry on our shoulders. Whatever it is, we need to learn to provide better support to those around us. Don's story shows both the rawness of grief after a loss and the importance of support through the process.

Don's Story

I had the opportunity to talk with Don, a pastor-missionary who suffered the loss of his beloved wife about a year and a half ago. During our conversation he shared that his feelings are still raw and his life has changed dramatically. His wife's cancer was misdiagnosed during the Covid-19 pandemic, and when they received the correct diagnosis, the cancer had already metastasized. She immediately underwent surgery in Cyprus but had to continue with chemotherapy as soon as possible, so they gave away everything in ten days and returned to the United States for treatment. The chemotherapy was difficult on her body, and she eventually lost her life.

Don describes his early days of mourning as very dark. He could not focus on Bible reading or prayer. All he could do was cry. He describes how he needed tissue boxes all over the house because of the constant tears he was shedding. All the crying wore him out, and he candidly shared how he now understands why some people could entertain suicide as a viable option because the pain he experienced was overwhelming.

I asked him what prayer looked like for him during this stage, and he said some days all he could do was groan and cry. Some days it was deep sighs from his heart. There were no words to express his grief and deep sorrow. He had been a Christian and pastor for many years and knew all the right theology, but as he put it, "There is also a very human side that experiences deep sadness." The unrealized life he had hoped to live out with his life partner, the memories, the gaping hole in his heart, and the loss of intimacy all contributed to this immense grief.

I asked him how his experience of lament helped him and how he found comfort during those times. Don shared several ways he found comfort. First, he knew in his heart that God knew his pain. This was especially comforting because he knew he was not alone. He said that his tears helped him to connect with God. Lament taught him how inadequate human language is. Words were inadequate to express his pain. Tears and groanings of the soul came closer to doing so, but ironically, silence was sometimes the best communication. He had walked a long time with God and knew God's voice. As he grieved, there was an inner witness he felt even in his deepest pain. He likened it to "locking eyes" with Jesus on the cross. While Don acknowledged that the pain Jesus suffered was so much more, he knew that Christ understood his pain. He did not see Jesus as his buddy or friend but rather as God who holds life in his hands. Don recounted how his times of prayer did not necessarily assure him that things were going to be all right, but rather he just needed to be still. Being in God's presence and knowing that God saw him brought him calm in the midst of his chaos.

Some days this stillness was exactly what he needed to just take the next step. He often proceeded minute by minute rather than day by day. Sometimes the next step was just getting out of bed and brushing his teeth. Other times it was getting the toast out of the toaster or putting on his shoes to take a walk so that he did not remain in bed and retreat into the darkness he felt in his heart. He described it as just muddling through. While things are still raw and even surreal for Don, he now finds that memories of his wife are becoming sweeter, and he recognizes that life will never be the same. He does not want to get over the loss because his wife shaped who he is today and he wants to honor that. He is navigating life with a new normal. In the past his wife was the one who always made the bed, but now he honors her by making the bed every morning, which he says also helps to bring a sense of order into his life. These small but significant steps are helping Don find comfort in his pain and loss.

Another way he found comfort was in his willing submission to God's ways. The tragic loss of his wife was not the first time Don lamented the loss of a loved one. In his late twenties, he and his wife lost their premature infant girl in Argentina. He recounts how he prayed to God, telling him that even though he did not know why his baby girl was taken, maybe in heaven he would find out. To his dismay, he heard God ask, even if in heaven Don does not find out why, would he still trust God? Don assented in his heart. He says there is also an act of will in our lament. Sometimes we need to just submit, surrender, and trust in God's ways. Like the psalmist after pouring out his heart, Don also recognized the importance of submitting to God and his ways because God is loving and kind. Even if we do not get the answers we want, God is still trustworthy.

Don found and continues to find comfort through community and certain individuals. The most helpful were those who just sat with him in silence. Conversely, those who kept asking him how he was doing or who tried to comfort him by offering reasons for his suffering were the least helpful. The last thing he wanted to do in his exhaustion was to explain over and over again his state or to hear trite reasons for his pain. He just needed friends to witness and understand his grief. It was those who had gone through deep suffering who brought him the most comfort. They did not even have to say much; he just knew that they knew his pain. Many of these individuals simply told him that it was good to see him and sat alongside him in his grief.

This time of suffering helped Don to appreciate the loving community that he had around him. There were countless individuals from his church who came by when his wife was struggling and brought meals. Don recalls a touching moment when a group of church members stopped by their home to pray outside for his wife. She was so moved and grateful that she mustered all her strength to greet and thank them. This was the last time his wife interacted with their church community.

After his wife's passing, individuals in the church allowed Don space to grieve but also welcomed him into the community. One Sunday school teacher and friend texted him every day for a month after his wife's passing. Don confessed that in the earlier stages, even with all his pastoral training, he did not navigate community life well. He felt ill-equipped to adjust to single life again. Don was not his same outgoing, gregarious self. He found chitchat very draining and did not enjoy being in large crowds. When he went to church, he did not know where to sit because he was now all alone. This is something not many people talk about. How does one navigate singleness after being in a marriage for so many years? Going to church was awkward, and many times he left right after the service.

In his earlier stages of grief, Don relied on two good friends who were great listeners, and he also sought out counseling and joined a grief recovery group. He confesses that he is now less judgmental toward those who struggle with deep pain and sorrow. Sometimes the most comforting words were those that simply encouraged him to keep trusting and believing what he already knew. One friend reminded Don of his clear understanding of life and afterlife in his younger years as a pastor and exhorted him to not lose that now during dark times.

While Don is grateful for the community around him, there were some in the church who were ill-equipped or uncomfortable with those who were grieving. Sadly, this experience is not uncommon. Unlike Don, who experienced many loving individuals in his church, I have also heard from countless people who did not find the church to be very comforting during times of grief. So, what can we do better?

How can we be a family and a place of refuge for those experiencing loss? I offer just a few practical steps. First, acknowledge the grief and pain but do not constantly bring it up. When we continue to bring up the situation, we can make people feel like compassion projects. Too often, when people are grieving, we either inundate them with attention or we completely ignore them because we want to give them space. Acknowledge and recognize the hurt but do not keep asking how they are feeling or doing. Give them the space to share when they are ready.

Another practical step is to invite those who are grieving to be a part of the community, even in their brokenness. Do not be offended if they are unable to respond well. Like Don, many who are grieving loss are still struggling to navigate life without their loved ones. Offer open arms and invitations to help them to feel a sense of belonging during this time of adjustment. They need to know that they are not forgotten, but they also need space to heal. Being mindful of those who are alone in church is crucial. It is often awkward and difficult to enter a space where everyone else seems to have their family and close-knit support groups. It is important to extend invitations as a sign of friendship, not as an act of pity. People who are grieving can tell the difference. Temporary acts of pity are not helpful.

Acts of service are also comforting. Cleaning someone's home or cooking a meal without expectations often communicates great care and concern. As Don shared, there were days he could not even get out of his bed, let alone clean his house or cook a meal. It took effort just to get up and brush his teeth. Acts of service during this time ministered to him greatly.

Don also noted that singing worship songs in church was particularly hard because of the lyrics. Incorporating time in the worship service that acknowledges those dealing with pain and suffering can help them to feel included. This affirms that they are welcome and not out of place. Choosing songs that speak of suffering and the ability to come to God with our raw emotions can be helpful in acknowledging that we do not come to church only when we have everything put together.

MOURNING IN THE BIBLE

As I close this second half of the book, I want to highlight two observations made by Xuan Huong Thi Pham in *Mourning in the Ancient Near East and the Hebrew Bible*.[4] The first concerns identifying with a mourner through participation in different rites, such as weeping, tearing clothes, sitting on the ground, sprinkling dust on the head, sitting in silence, and shaving the head and/or beard. Pham points out that these were all public acts that could be seen and heard by everyone and were readily recognizable.

While we may not tear our clothes or sprinkle dust on our heads today, we can still publicly acknowledge to both the mourner and others that we are suffering with them. Perhaps the most contemporary way this is illustrated is when people wear a pink bow to show their support for breast cancer and those who have died from it. Another example is how people tie yellow ribbons around their trees as a symbol of remembrance of men and women who served in the military far from home. By doing this gesture, they show the world that they are remembering someone. We may not always have to be so visible in showing our solidarity with those who are suffering or waiting, but perhaps we need to be more deliberate in how we show others that we stand with them in their pain. These obvious physical acts allow sufferers to know that they are not alone, that they have a community that supports them. These gestures may be as simple as weeping with those who are suffering, sitting with them in silence, or even fasting and praying for them as they grieve. More overt options may be wearing a flower that the person who passed loved or wearing their favorite color. Whatever physical act is adopted, it should be something that mourners recognize, find significant, and appreciate.

Pham also observes that comfort was offered through speaking to mourners and providing advice on how to move on from their pain. These words should be spoken with discernment concerning both the content and timing. We want to be sure that we are not rushing people

---

[4]Xuan Huong Thi Pham, *Mourning in the Ancient Near East and the Hebrew Bible* (Sheffield: Sheffield Academic, 2000), 28.

in their grief and that they are ready to move forward. Perhaps those who have gone through suffering are the best to provide this type of support. If you have gone through deep suffering, remember that your experiences can be a place of deep ministry for those who are currently dealing with loss and grief. Your pain and testimony can help others know that they are not alone. Paul states in 2 Corinthians 1:3-4, "Blessed be the God and Father of our Lord Jesus Christ, the Father of mercies and God of all comfort, who comforts us in all our affliction, so that we may be able to comfort those who are in any affliction, with the comfort with which we ourselves are comforted by God" (ESV).

Whichever steps you take to comfort and identify with those who are grieving, know that it may not always go the way you plan or be received in the way you hoped. Be encouraged that your efforts are never in vain when you do it as unto the Lord. Grief is messy, and it takes great patience to love and support those who are walking through it.

REFLECTION QUESTIONS

1. Have you recently lost a loved one? How have you been processing the death of your loved one? Are you isolating yourself? Are you trying to numb the pain in other ways?
2. How can we lament a situation of loss without becoming hopeless?
3. How have you experienced comfort from your community and from the Lord during your grief?
4. How can the church be a family and place of refuge for those experiencing loss and pain? What are a few ways the church can do a better job supporting those who are grieving?

INDIVIDUAL PRACTICE

Do not let your pain isolate you when you are grieving. When you are ready, think about what next steps you need to take. Is it to put on your shoes and take a walk? Is it to call a friend? Is it to join a grief recovery group? Ask the Lord for strength to take the next step and to establish a new normal in your life.

CORPORATE PRACTICE

You or your church can establish a ministry team that specifically focuses on acts of service for families that have lost a loved one. Perhaps they can help set up rotations for meals, housecleaning, visitations, babysitting, and so on. This will alleviate discomfort for those wanting to serve but unsure how and can help those who are grieving with practical daily needs.

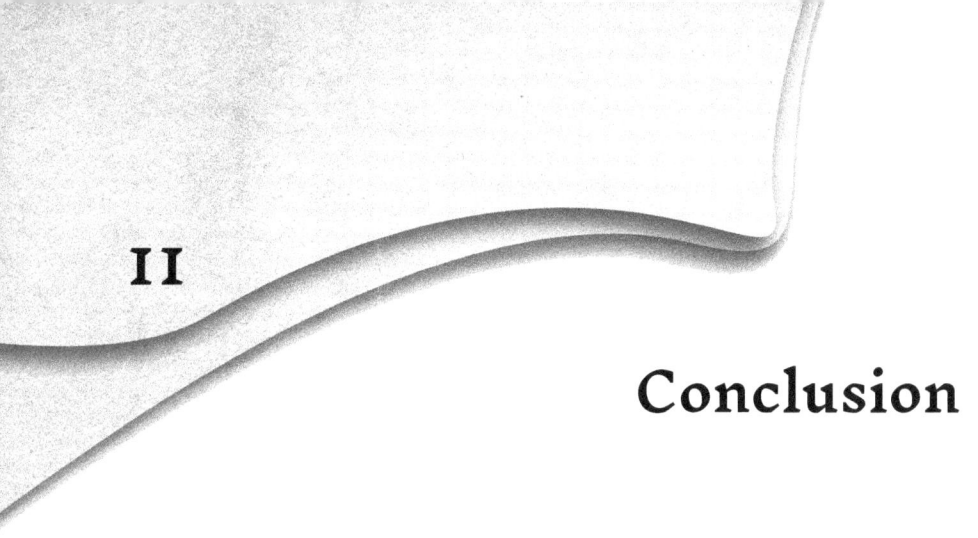

11

Conclusion

Recovering biblical lament is more than just grasping the concept. It is learning from Scripture and letting the genre of lament inform our practice. As we find ourselves dealing with the uncertainty and suffering that surround us, let us remember the following important points:

- Lament is a necessary part of the process of grieving and healing.
- While ancient Near Eastern cultures practiced lament, biblical lament is different because it appeals to a God who knows us, cares, and acts on our behalf.
- Lament is something we do not do alone.
- Lament is not just one emotion or a uniform response.
- Even when God does not act on this side of eternity, lament helps us to move through life with hope.

LAMENT IS A NECESSARY PART OF THE PROCESS OF GRIEVING AND HEALING

When we are experiencing pain, doubt, and other forms of grief and suffering, we must fight the tendency to ignore, suppress, or deny these emotions. Instead, we need to be like the psalmists and bring our pain before God and lament in his presence. Giving voice to our pain strengthens our intimacy with God and invites our Great Physician to heal and speak into these situations. Psalm 107:19-20 speaks to this: "Then they cried to the Lord in their trouble, and he saved them from their distress. He sent out his word and healed them; he rescued them from the grave." Through the practice of lament, we express our dependence on God and ask him to intervene.

Additionally, when we allow ourselves to feel these emotions, we are taking a step toward greater resilience. Scientific research also supports this claim. For instance, a recent study of university students post-Covid-19 found that expressive writing through the practice of journaling resulted in an increase in resilience after weathering the pandemic.[1] Whether we journal, pray aloud, pray silently, or express our pain through other creative avenues, the practice of lament is critical for us to move toward healing and resilience in the midst of our pain and grief. I know that this is not easy. Sometimes acknowledging our pain and feeling these emotions is extremely uncomfortable. However, when we face it with God, we recognize that we are not alone. Our feelings are valid, but we can also allow God's truth to shine into our darkness.

WHILE ANCIENT NEAR EASTERN CULTURES PRACTICED LAMENT, BIBLICAL LAMENT IS DIFFERENT

Biblical lament is distinct from lament as practiced by other ancient Near Eastern cultures. Yahweh, the God of the Bible, is not distant. As Psalm 34:18 says, "The Lord is close to the brokenhearted and saves those who are crushed in spirit." We do not have to come before his presence to butter him up so that he will listen to our request. As New Testament believers, we can come before his throne with confidence when we need help and mercy (Heb 4:16). Our Heavenly Father knows the very number of hairs on our heads (Lk 12:7). We do not have to introduce ourselves to him or ask for someone else to intercede for us. We also do not have to recite any formulas or incantations for God to act; we can simply come before him in honesty and vulnerability.

The prophet Isaiah reminds us, "Since ancient times no one has heard, no ear has perceived, no eye has seen any God besides you, who acts on behalf of those who wait for him" (Is 64:4). When we practice biblical

---

[1] Max S. Lohner and Carmela Aprea, "The Resilience Journal: Exploring the Potential of Journal Interventions to Promote Resilience in University Students," *Frontiers in Psychology* 12 (2021): 702683.

lament, we are waiting on God, who cares and acts on behalf of his people. Our waiting is not passive but active. We wait in expectation for what God will do. To be sure, how God acts may not be what we expect or on our timing, but we can be confident that he always acts for our good. Romans 8:32 says, "He who did not spare his own Son, but gave him up for us all—how will he not also, along with him, graciously give us all things?" Let us lay down our burdens and trust that he hears us and has the best intentions for our future.

LAMENT IS SOMETHING WE DO NOT DO ALONE

The Bible has both individual and communal/corporate laments. We are not called to practice lament only by ourselves. There will be times when we will need to lament as a community, whether to stand against injustice for those who are weak and voiceless or to stand in solidarity to support those who are experiencing pain, grief, or loss. We are not to live the Christian life as lone rangers. We are called to care for one another. Galatians 6:2 reminds us, "Carry each other's burdens, and in this way you will fulfill the law of Christ." We must be careful not to turn away from those who are hurting because it is uncomfortable; instead, we need to press in and let them know that they are not alone. I am reminded of an old proverb that says, "A joy shared is doubled, but a grief shared is halved." In other words, we lighten the load for one another when we share our burdens. May we be part of churches that provide refuge and healing for the oppressed and broken. In this way we will reflect the ministry of Christ.

LAMENT IS NOT JUST ONE EMOTION OR A UNIFORM RESPONSE

The practice of lament is not only for times of sadness or grief, but for when we are feeling lonely, angry, guilty, hopeless, in pain, and depressed. It is for times of sickness, loneliness, repentance, abandonment, injustice, and loss. The Psalms provide examples from all of these situations. As we have observed, biblical lament is not a flat, one-dimensional concept. It is a fully orbed practice that arises from the genre of lament. It also does not stop at expressions of sadness or crying, but encompasses the journey we need to walk when life becomes overwhelming and painful.

Lament will not always look the same. For some, lament is sitting in silence, like Job and his friends. For others, it is to express themselves in song, like the psalmist. For still others it is honest expressions of doubt and questions, like Habakkuk. God can handle all our anger, questions, and pain. If we can express these deep emotions with our closest friends, why can we not do so before the Lord? Whatever the situation, biblical lament is an act of faith. Instead of turning away from God, we choose to engage him.

It may be that life is filled with more difficulties and losses than wins. Perhaps that is why there are more lament psalms than any other genre type in the Psalter. If this is the case, then we must learn to practice lament even more. While our intimacy with God can be built through the wins in life, but most often, it grows when we walk through suffering, hopelessness, and grief.

LAMENT HELPS US MOVE THROUGH LIFE WITH HOPE

There are situations we face in life that are unalterable. For example, the loss of a loved one is final on this side of eternity. There are other times when the practice of lament does not result in God acting to bring the change we had desired. This does not mean that we are without hope. In these situations, our practice of lament can draw us closer to God as we are reminded that the ultimate hope in life is not necessarily found here and now. God gives the grace and strength we need for each day. Paul lamented the thorn that God did not take away, but God told Paul that his grace was sufficient. Paul learned to see God's strength in his own suffering. He expresses this in 2 Corinthians 12:9-10: "'My grace is sufficient for you, for my power is made perfect in weakness.' Therefore I will boast all the more gladly about my weaknesses, so that Christ's power may rest on me. That is why, for Christ's sake, I delight in weaknesses, in insults, in hardships, in persecutions, in difficulties. For when I am weak, then I am strong." Though God may not always respond in the way we want, we can be sure that he will provide the strength we need. We can also know that "our light and momentary troubles are achieving for us an eternal glory that far outweighs them all" (2 Cor 4:17). God never promises to give us all we want, but he promises to give us what we need in this life and even more in the next. Ultimately lament often leads us to realize that what we truly need is him. Perhaps this is why so many have experienced greater intimacy and hope in the midst of pain and dire circumstances that should have rendered them hopeless.

As I conclude this book, I want to take us to a passage in the Old Testament that shows us that lament not only leads us to greater hope but also helps us to find our strength in God when we have no strength. First Samuel 30:3-6 tells us about a time in David's life when he lost everything.

> When David and his men reached Ziklag, they found it destroyed by fire and their wives and sons and daughters taken captive. So David and his men wept aloud until they had no strength left to weep. David's two wives had been captured—Ahinoam of Jezreel and Abigail, the widow of Nabal of Carmel. David was greatly distressed because the men were talking of stoning him; each one was bitter in spirit because of his sons and daughters. But David found strength in the Lord his God.

In these verses, David and his men come back to their camp only to find that it has been raided by the Amalekites. All the men engage in lament together because their shared loss is so heavy. They reach a point where they do not even have strength left to weep. Further, David is "greatly distressed" because some of his own close friends want to stone him. Perhaps they were looking for a scapegoat. The community that mutually supported him and wept with him has now turned against him. He has nowhere else to go.

The text says that David "found strength in the Lord his God." This verb appears in the reflexive form of the verb *ḥāzaq*, "to be strong," meaning David "strengthened himself." The strength he found was not just downloaded into his spirit by God. He had to come before God and interact with God through lament. He strengthened himself in the Lord. While the text does not explicitly call this lament, the context shows that David is experiencing emotional pain from loss, abandonment, betrayal, and unjust accusations. He turns to the only place he can in his "great distress." This turning is characterized by his reflexive action of strengthening himself in the Lord. In other words, this required effort on David's part. David did not just sit there. He pressed into the Lord, put effort in his seeking and strengthening. He also did not give into despair, nor did he just continue to weep hopelessly. No, he came into God's presence and processed this great distress before him.

This passage offers us a picture of how lament is not just about grieving and venting. No, it is so much more. It is a way for us to pour out our hearts, complaints, doubts, shame, injustices, and more in order to find strength in the Lord. David does not find his strength in the hope that he is going to receive his family back. No, that does not happen until later. At the time of his lament, he does not know whether that will be the outcome; nevertheless, he finds strength in God.

If David is indeed the author of many of the laments in Psalms, perhaps he is giving us a glimpse into how he strengthened himself in the Lord here in 1 Samuel. The Lord hears our cries and helps us through our difficulties. Strength and deliverance may not come in the way we expect or in the timing we want, but God is always faithful. Ultimately our hope is in God and not in the circumstances of this life. When we press into God during difficult times, he gives us the strength and hope to take one more step forward as we walk with him through our darkest valleys. May you be encouraged to seek the Lord in whatever circumstances you are facing in this season of life and may the practice of biblical lament strengthen you and give you greater hope in the Lord.

Scripture Index

Old Testament

Genesis
3, *59*
3:1, *106*
4:9, *126*
12:1, *89*
12:1-3, *114*
18:25, *129*
50:10, *160*

Exodus
3:7-8, *55, 169*
5:22-23, *99*
15–17, *21*
15:11, *153*
16:28, *101*
19–24, *89*
20, *126*
22:22-23, *123*
34, *87*
34:6, *87, 106, 152*
34:6-7, *110*
34:7, *87*

Leviticus
11:32, *88*
19:18, *115*
19:34, *115*

Numbers
14–17, *21*
14:11, *101*

Deuteronomy
5, *126*
10:18, *123*
24:19, *123*
28:15-68, *168*
29:22-28, *53*
32:4, *152*
32:25, *106*
33:2-5, *120*
34:7, *104*

Joshua
2:12, *126*
18:3, *101*

Ruth
1:8-9, *126*

1 Samuel
24, *116*
26:1-25, *116*
30:3-6, *185*

2 Samuel
1, *30*
1:17, *15, 160*
1:17-27, *116*
3:33, *15, 160*
11–12, *84*
19:16-23, *116*

1 Kings
8:46-51, *83*

2 Kings
20:3, *149*
20:5, *149*
25:1-21, *161*

2 Chronicles
7:14, *91*
20:3-5, *27*

Job
2:9, *69*
3, *4*
3:11, *99*
12:24, *99*
16:7-14, *151*
18:2, *101*
19:2, *101*
41–42:6, *110*

Psalms
1–41, *135*
1–50, *84*
1:1-3, *125*
1:2, *24*
2, *18, 84*
3, *19, 27*
3–7, *19*
4:1, *20*
5–7, *19, 27*
5:8, *27*
6, *11, 81, 145*
6:2, *21*
6:2-4, *22*
6:5, *28*
6:6, *27*
7:6, *22*
9:2, *20*
9:8, *24*
11, *19*
12, *112*
13, *19, 27, 100, 101, 102, 103, 110*

13:1, *100*
13:2, *101, 104*
13:2-3, *101*
13:3, *104, 105*
13:4, *105*
13:5, *105, 106*
13:6, *26, 107*
17, *19, 27*
17:1-5, *22*
17:15, *23*
18, *18*
20–21, *18*
20:3, *37*
20:7, *24*
22, *19, 27, 128*
22–23, *19*
22:1, *100*
22:1-2, *128*
22:1-5, *110*
22:4-5, *22*
22:7, *27*
22:19-21, *28*
22:22, *56*
23:4, *7, 129*
23:5, *34*
25–26, *19, 27*
25:11, *22*
27–28, *19*
27:7-14, *19, 27*
27:10, *53*
28, *19, 27*
28:1, *28, 150*
28:2, *27*
29, *92*
30–32, *19*
30:4, *150*
30:11, *26*
31, *19, 27*
31:11-12, *21*
31:15, *27*
32, *81*
33:4, *152*
33:18, *105*
34:18, *182*
35, *19, 27*
35:12-14, *116*
38, *27, 76, 81, 145*
38–39, *19, 27*
39, *76*
41, *19*
41:9, *128*
42, *133, 137*

42–43, *2, 19, 27, 132, 136, 143*
42–72, *135*
42:1, *138*
42:2, *139*
42:2-3, *136*
42:3, *132, 136*
42:4, *136, 137*
42:5, *132, 138, 139*
42:7, *137*
42:8-9, *138*
42:9, *138, 139*
42:10, *132, 136, 138*
42:11, *132, 138, 139*
43, *134, 138*
43:1, *138*
43:1-2, *138*
43:2, *138*
43:3, *139, 141*
43:3-4, *136*
43:4, *139, 141*
43:4-5, *138*
43:5, *132, 139*
44, *19, 25, 26, 27, 76*
44:4-8, *27*
45, *18*
50:12-13, *37*
51, *19, 27, 42, 81, 84, 97, 98*
51–100, *88, 92, 120, 126, 127, 149, 150*
51:1-3, *21*
51:2, *87, 88, 91*
51:2-3, *88*
51:3, *91*
51:3-11, *86*
51:4, *89*
51:4-6, *91*
51:5, *89*
51:6, *86*
51:9, *88*
51:11-12, *88*
51:14-15, *93*
51:16, *91, 92*
51:16-17, *47*
51:17, *91*
51:18-19, *37*
54–57, *19, 27*
54:1, *20*
54:6, *37, 47*
55:16, *23, 124*
55:23, *23, 124*
56:12, *47*
56:12-13, *26*

57, *19*
57:1, *22*
58, *112*
59, *19, 27*
59:1-4, *21*
60, *19, 76*
60:6-8, *24*
61, *19, 27*
61:8, *47*
63, *19*
63–64, *19, 27*
68:5, *35, 123*
68:6, *142*
69, *19, 112, 113*
69–71, *19, 27*
69:1, *22*
69:1-3, *129*
69:2, *28*
69:4-5, *27*
69:19-20, *21*
69:25, *113*
69:30-31, *37*
71, *19*
71:14-24, *28*
71:18, *56*
72, *18*
73–89, *135*
73:2, *125*
73:4-10, *21*
74, *19, 27*
74:13-14, *35*
74:13-17, *27*
77, *19*
77:11-15, *100*
77:12, *24*
79–80, *19*
79:2-3, *159*
80, *27, 76*
80:8-11, *27*
80:12, *103*
81:6-10, *24*
83, *19, 112*
84, *27*
85, *19*
85:1-3, *27*
86, *19, 27*
86:1-4, *22*
88, *19, 25, 27, 41, 76, 145, 146, 152, 157, 172*
88–89, *38, 42*
88:1, *147, 148, 149*
88:1-2, *151*

Scripture Index

88:3, *150*
88:3-4, *28, 150*
88:3-6, *153*
88:3-9, *21*
88:4, *150*
88:5, *150*
88:6, *150*
88:7, *150, 153*
88:8, *150, 153*
88:9, *152*
88:10-11, *37*
88:10-12, *152*
88:12, *153*
88:13, *152, 153*
88:15-18, *151*
89, *27, 41, 42, 76*
90, *76*
90–91, *19*
90–106, *135*
94, *19, 112, 118, 120, 127, 130*
94:1, *120*
94:2, *120, 121, 123*
94:3, *121, 123, 124*
94:3-7, *121, 123*
94:3-11, *122*
94:4, *124*
94:5, *121, 122*
94:5-6, *123*
94:6, *121*
94:7, *121, 123, 124*
94:8, *124*
94:9-10, *124*
94:10, *124*
94:11, *124*
94:12-13, *125*
94:12-15, *124*
94:13, *125*
94:14, *125*
94:15, *122, 125, 127*
94:16-17, *125*
94:16-19, *125*
94:16-22, *122*
94:16-23, *125*
94:17, *126*
94:18, *125, 126, 127*
94:19, *125*
94:21, *126*
94:22, *125, 126, 127*
94:23, *122, 127*
101, *18*
102, *19, 27, 81, 145*
102–103, *19*
102:11, *28*
103:14, *105*
104:20-30, *33*
106:6, *54*
107–150, *135*
107:19-20, *181*
109, *19, 27, 112*
109:4-5, *116*
109:7-9, *24*
109:8, *113*
110, *18*
115:4-8, *36*
120, *19, 27*
123, *19*
126, *19*
126:5-6, *73*
129, *112*
130, *19, 27, 81, 83*
132, *18*
137, *19, 112*
137:8-9, *112*
139:16, *53*
140–143, *19, 27*
143, *81*
143:1, *20*
144:1-11, *18*
146:9, *123*
150, *22*

Proverbs
3:13-17, *125*
8:32-36, *125*
17:5, *171*
21:3, *56*
25:21, *116*
26:27, *125*

Ecclesiastes
1:1, *124*

Isaiah
1:27, *153*
10:1-34, *123*
25:1, *153*
26:3, *142*
33:10-13, *24*
38:9-20, *148*
38:21, *148*
40, *110*
40:11, *142*
40:12-31, *106*
41:10, *156, 158*
46:13, *153*
64:4, *182*
64:4-5, *142*
66:11, *126*

Jeremiah
2:22, *88*
11:18-20, *4*
16:7, *126*
20:7-8, *100*
31:15, *160*
47:6, *101*
48:17, *168*
52, *161*

Lamentations
1, *66, 160, 162, 163, 167, 172*
1:1, *167, 168*
1:2, *66, 168*
1:3, *168*
1:3-5, *168*
1:4, *168*
1:5, *168*
1:7, *168, 170*
1:8, *168*
1:8-10, *168*
1:9, *66, 167, 168, 169*
1:10-11, *169*
1:11, *167*
1:12, *66, 170*
1:12-16, *167*
1:12-22, *167*
1:14, *170*
1:15, *167, 170*
1:16, *170*
1:16-17, *168*
1:17, *66, 170*
1:18, *83, 170*
1:18-19, *167, 170*
1:19, *170*
1:20, *170*
1:20-22, *167*
1:21, *66, 168, 170, 171*
1:21-22, *171*
2, *162*
2:1-9, *151*
3, *19, 162*
4, *162*
5, *9, 19, 162*
5:7, *159*
5:22, *25*

Ezekiel
26:17, *168*
27:32, *15, 160*

Daniel
9:18, *74*

Hosea
4, *53*
10:5, *83*

Amos
5:17, *83*

Micah
6:6-8, *37, 38*

Habakkuk
1, *4, 72, 75, 100*
1:2, *101*
1:2-4, *72*
1:13, *75*
1:17, *72*
3, *75*
3:1-19, *72*
3:16-18, *107*

Malachi
3:5, *123*

NEW TESTAMENT

Matthew
2:18, *160*
5:3-12, *125*
5:44, *113*
6:9-13, *20*
6:10, *72*
11:2-24, *115*
11:28, *61*
23:13-39, *115*
27:45-46, *15*

Mark
15:34, *15*

Luke
6:27, *113*
7:36-50, *94*
7:47-48, *94*
11:1-4, *20*
12:1, *82*
12:7, *105, 182*
18:1-18, *121*
18:4, *121*
18:7-8, *121*
24:13-35, *100*
24:17, *69*
24:19, *69*
24:19-24, *69*
24:27, *69*
24:32, *69*

John
2:17, *113*
6:68, *25*
11:15, *100*
11:17-32, *15*
12:1-7, *15*
15:1-4, *148*
15:4, *149*
15:7, *149*
20:24-28, *100*

Acts
1:16-20, *113*
8:2, *61*
8:20-21, *115*
13:10-11, *115*
20:38, *61*

Romans
2:4, *87*
7:7-25, *83*
8:28, *6*
8:31, *106*
8:32, *106, 107, 183*
8:32-34, *55*
8:32-39, *110*
8:35-39, *140*
12:17-21, *117*
13:1-4, *117*

1 Corinthians
5:1-8, *83*
12:26, *8*

2 Corinthians
1:3-4, *179*
4:17, *185*
6:16, *54*
7:10, *83*
12:8, *4*
12:9-10, *57, 184*

Galatians
1:8, *115*
3:29, *116*
6:2, *183*

Ephesians
6:17, *140*

2 Timothy
2:1-12, *117*
3:16, *114*
4:14, *115*

Hebrews
4:15, *105*
4:15-16, *70*
4:16, *21, 70, 88, 105, 182*
7:27, *83*
10:19, *54*
10:19-23, *110*
13:5, *106*

James
1:2, *75*
4:6-10, *92*
4:8, *72*
5:16, *83*

1 Peter
5:6, *142*
5:7, *105*

1 John
1:9, *83*

Revelation
6:9-11, *115*
19:15, *120*